Reality Sells

Reality Sells
How to Bring Customers Back Again and Again by Marketing Your Genuine Story

Written by
Andrew Corbus
and
Bill Guertin

WBusiness
Books

an imprint of New Win Publishing
a division of Academic Learning Company, LLC

Library of Congress Cataloging-in-Publication Data

Corbus, Andrew.
    Reality sells: how to bring customers back again and again by marketing your
genuine story/by Andrew Corbus and Bill Guertin.
        p. cm.
    ISBN 978-0-8329-5008-7
    1. Advertising. 2. Marketing. 3. Customer services. 4. Consumer satisfaction.
I. Guertin, Bill. II. Title.
    HF5823.C59733 2007
    658.8–dc22

2007014627

Table of Contents

For more information and the latest on *Reality Sells*, visit:
www.realitysells.com.

Foreword
by
Ivan Burnell

At last, a book presenting and promoting the concept of honesty in marketing and selling. This closely held secret to wealth has finally been revealed! *Tell the truth, the whole truth and nothing but the truth.* It's a lesson I discovered in my own career many years ago.

Due to a set of life circumstances, I was without a job, stone broke and owing tens of thousands of dollars to various merchants. That is when I was offered a job as a salesman, selling life insurance, and I would be paid while I was learning the trade. The agency took me on, trained me, helped me get my license and sent me out in the field to work using the formula, words and technique that they taught me.

I worked hard and long, studying different products, trying different markets, going to motivational seminars, and always wanting to be a better agent. Yet I was barely making a living, and certainly not paying back my debts. Friends told me to leave my small hometown in the hills of New Hampshire to a big city where the high rollers and successful insurance agents were, but I did not want to leave the area.

Then one day, after a particularly unsuccessful sales appointment, I was ready to quit because I could no longer continue to put up with the frustration and tension of trying to get people to buy life insurance. That is when I had my awakening. I had been trying to manipulate people into buying something that they did not necessarily want to buy and I did not feel comfortable doing it.

From that point on, I changed my approach and became real, and made my sales efforts all about the customer. Within two years I became the top agent in my company, I was able to pay off all my debts, and was offered a management position, all while staying in the small town that I loved. By using the techniques that you're about to read, I discovered what you're about to discover for yourself: "Reality Sells." It really does!

If you follow the precepts of this book, you cannot fail to become a success, whatever your product, wherever you are.

Ivan Burnell, Author

"Power of Positive Doing", "Say Yes to Life", "Road to a Happier Marriage."

Acknowledgements

A project like this cannot be realized without the profound influence of others. We are grateful for all the great mentors we have each had throughout the years. As we worked through our ideas, and mined our own knowledge and experiences, a number of business and life lessons were incorporated into our writing. We recognize the wisdom of previous employers, business partners, teachers, coaches and mentors from weeks, years, and even decades ago. We have both been blessed with having great examples in life.

We are particularly grateful to the friends and mentors in the speaking and training industry who have been very gracious with their time and knowledge. In very few places have we found a greater example of mentorship.

Thank you to our families and wives, Sherri and Jessica for your support, encouragement and understanding; we truly couldn't have done this without you.

We dedicate this book to all who give freely of themselves for the benefit of others by serving as teachers, coaches, and mentors.

Introduction

Andrew Corbus   As a small-business owner, I was given a thoughtful holiday gift by Glendal Kilbride, my radio-advertising sales rep. It was a book titled *The Wizard of Ads* by Roy H. Williams. Knowing my personality, she believed that I would be able to identify with it.

I was intrigued by Roy's book, which had much to say about advertising and how to improve its effectiveness. Because of his insight, I began to look for new ways to deepen my radio effectiveness. Glendal put me in touch with Bill Guertin, the station's sales director, to work out some of my ideas.

Bill and I began to meet on a regular basis, sharing marketing ideas and stories. The result of these meetings, over the course of a number of years, is the information contained in this book.

We wrote it because we both realized how difficult it was to come up with real advertising copy that wasn't like everything else. We also felt as though business owners spent little or no time educating staff members about advertising, and we couldn't believe how much money was spent on advertising that wasn't supported with customer-service training.

It's been a fun ride. Thanks, Glendal, for giving me the book; and thank you, Roy, for giving us something to meet about in the first place.

Bill Guertin   It has always been a goal of mine to write a book, but I've held off for several years because I wanted to be sure to write something others would consider worthy of reading. I'm glad I waited until now.

Reality Sells is the culmination of many thoughts, observations, and real-life trial and error that Andy and I have shared in the business and advertising world. We believe there's not another business book like it.

You'll see several sidebars throughout the text that we have created to give you our own personal revelations that are relevant to the topics being discussed. You'll see my "800-Pound Insights," which are my experiences, thoughts, and comments, along with Andrew's "Authenticity Points," his personal stories and thoughts that add to the subject matter.

One other special feature throughout the book is a group of sections called "Reality Check." These are valuable opportunities to reflect, study, and work on your particular business situation. In my mind, the ultimate compliment to a book is to have someone say, "Your work really made me think." We believe you'll find several of those moments inside.

Thank you for the privilege you've given us to make a potential impact in your business life. We think you'll enjoy it.

CHAPTER 1
The Start of the Revolution

People want to be real. Customers want real service. Businesses are trying to be real.

But why?

Where is all this reality coming from?

It all started innocently enough.

It was 1996, and Charlie Parsons and Bob Geldof were toying with a new television concept. It was a stretch: Put sixteen people on a deserted-island location, divide them into survival teams, have them compete in several sports-like challenges, and vote one person off the island at a time. Eventually the two teams would merge, and individuals would then compete against each other, with one person winning a large grand prize.

The idea was loosely based on the novel *Robinson Crusoe,* and the resulting concept was a weekly series they named *Expedition Robinson*—an unscripted, dramatic production with cameras stuck everywhere on the island, and amateurs as the "stars." Parsons and Geldof struck a deal with the Swedish public-television station SVT, and filming began in the summer of 1997.

No one could have predicted what would happen next.

When *Expedition Robinson* first aired, the Swedish media were extremely critical of the show, calling it "crap television" and "humiliating." It stirred a national debate in Sweden about what constituted moral and ethical television. As debate about the program raged on, viewership climbed each week. The more that people talked about it, the more people who watched it. The country was at once fascinated and outraged by this new form of entertainment.

After the program had aired for only a few weeks, a tragedy almost forced the show off the air; the very first person who was voted off the island was found dead in his own apartment, an apparent suicide. The family of the young man claimed that the public's rejection of him led to his decision to take his own life. That fact was never proven, but the incident fanned the flames of controversy even more, and ratings continued to climb.

Ultimately, 33-year-old Martin Melen was crowned the first-ever reality-show champion in the fall of 1997. *Expedition Robinson* would go on for several more seasons, and became the most-watched television program in Swedish history in its fourth year.

The revolution had begun.

Why Reality Is In

Like it or not, reality television has become the new norm of pop culture. *Survivor, Big Brother,* MTV's *The Real World, Fear Factor, American Idol, Dancing with the Stars, The Apprentice, The Biggest Loser, The Contender,* and dozens of other similar programs have become ratings superstars, each one a derivative of the original concept. The objective is eerily similar: Get people to do things on camera that are unscripted, unpredictable, and that eventually show their true colors.

We got a glimpse of this high-stakes reality in 1990, when *America's Funniest Home Videos* gave people an opportunity to expose their own dubious home-video tapings for a cool $10,000 grand prize. High ratings for the show and its popular host, sitcom star Bob Saget, got the network executives' wheels turning.

Fast-forward to today's reality TV landscape. Million-dollar cash prizes can now make winners both rich and famous. It's great to be on TV, but now it's about big money and big fame. With that much at stake, who *doesn't* want to be a millionaire?

The amazing part to most of us is the fact that these contestants are willing to expose themselves—faults and all—to all of America and the world. The chance to be the talk of the nation is the motivation behind shows like *Wife Swap* and *The Nanny*. Yes, they're paid to be a part of the program, but the real payoff for them is being on national TV.

Whether it's individuals vying for a million-dollar prize, or a Christian mom surviving a week with an atheist family, there is a fascination for the unvarnished truth that is capturing the interest of entertainment consumers worldwide. If you keep the camera on long enough, you eventually find out what these people are really like…and that's what the world wants to know.

It's now true in business as well. Customers also want to know what *you're* really like.

Consumers are sick to death of being lied to, sold to, and manipulated. They now want to know the true you. They want the authentic story, and they're much wiser to the tricks and empty promises of most of the advertising that's produced. In fact, they're finding more and more ways to get the inside scoop about your business without your help. Behind your back. In ways that you have absolutely no control over. And consumers are in love with these new means of communication.

Blogs, IM, and Texting: Today's New Billboards

It used to be that you had more control of the messages that customers saw and heard about you. Not anymore. There are now a number of ways to get the real scoop on whose business is hot and whose is not.

Want to know what young people are thinking these days? Go to *www.myspace.com*, *www.xanga.com*, or any of the other personal blogs available for everyone to see.

Blogging and instant messaging (IM) has all but replaced face-to-face conversation in many circles, spawning a new language of shortcut words and phrases (LOL, BRB, ROTF, etc.). And when these technology users are not at their computers, they're on cell phones texting messages back and forth.

What do these bloggers, IM'ers, and texters talk about? Anything and everything. Their businesses, their relationships, their feelings, their emotions, and their opinions on every detail of their lives. This is *their* voice, and they want to be heard. It's word of mouth to the millionth power. The Website *www.cluetrain.com* puts it this way:

> "Networked markets are beginning to self-organize faster than the companies that have traditionally served them. Thanks to the Web, markets are becoming better informed, smarter, and more demanding of qualities missing from most business organizations."

This is the new landscape of personal opinion, where products are made or broken, where trends can be praised or laid to waste, and where movies are hailed or trashed before they even make it to their opening weekend. Those who read these opinions are more willing to believe their peers than any newspaper ad, because those who write such comments aren't being paid to do so. The power has shifted to the people, and the people have more ways to share their opinions with the masses.

Gone are the days where all you needed to do was advertise a few polished words and slick sentences, and people would flock to your door in droves. Your reputation—and your ultimate success—is now literally in the hands of those you serve.

So who can win in a business atmosphere that you can't control?

You can.

If you know exactly who you are, deliver a clear, honest business message, and back up that message by providing the products or services you offer in the way in which you promised, you can win. Put more succinctly, it's "know thyself, promote thyself honestly, and do as thou sayeth every time."

This is the new language of business success, and its name is Authenticity.

 800-Pound Insight

My wife and I were on a weekend trip to Clearwater Beach, Florida, where we met a vendor of handmade jewelry at a craft fair. Sherri had never had an ankle bracelet, and she fell in love with one of the vendor's unique silver-beaded creations.

"How much?" I asked, fearing the worst.

Without hesitating, he shot out a price that I didn't think was too bad. "You'll see dozens of jewelry vendors here on the pier," he said, "but there's no one who'll sell you this kind of quality for that kind of price. I guarantee everything I sell for life. If you don't like it after you've worn it for a year, send it back, and I'll give you every penny back. If you love it and if it ever breaks, I'll send you a brand-new one for free."

This was too good to be true, I thought to myself. "How will we find you if we need you?"

He pulled out his card, which I will never forget.

The business card of Robert Jay Polukoff (pronounced Paula-Cough) is packed with information in small black letters on a plain-white card, but it is fabulous information. In big, bold letters across the middle, it reads:

100% SATISFACTION MONEY BACK GUARANTEE

In smaller letters, he then has his name (with the correct pronunciation) and his title: "Lapidary Genius Extraordinaire and Master Craftsman."

In the top-left corner, his card reads: "If you like them now, you will love them ten minutes from now—they always look new." (By the way, he was right.)

In the top right: "Real jewelry that's real treasure for less money than real trash." (He was right on that too. I passed the other vendors and didn't see half the quality he had, and all of them were substantially more expensive.)

The bottom right has his contact information along with the phrase: "Planned my work, working my plan." (Don't you want to do business with someone who has a plan? I do.)

The bottom left is my favorite part: "Coolest human to do business with. High-quality treasure at low price. Fix it for free for a lifetime. Built to last a lifetime the first time."

I have yet to take him up on his offer, because several years later, it's still Sherri's favorite piece of jewelry. I've seen and heard all those superlatives before, but I have never seen someone back them up like Robert Jay Polukoff. He is as authentic as they come.

Something as simple as a business card can create a lasting impression. I was so impressed with the card and the service that I have kept it for reference for several years. Robert chose to create a long-lasting calling card that would build confidence and remind people of the details of their experience. I look forward to doing business with Robert again, and I'm sure some of you do as well.

 Free Goodie

Want to contact Robert? For his contact information go to the Goodie Box at *www.realitysells.com* and enter the word ROBERT in the box. Note: You will need to register if you are a first time user.

Authenticity: What Customers Want

Ever done business with a company that advertised "fast, friendly service," and it wasn't fast, friendly, OR service?

As consumers, all we want is for somebody to do what they say they're going to do. If a dry cleaner advertises same-day shirts to be done by 4:00 p.m., we expect them to be true to their word. If a realtor says she can get you the best price for your home and will advertise it every week, anything less is a disappointment.

That's called being Authentic.

The language of reality in business is Authenticity. Not just saying it, but living it out.

In business, we believe Authenticity occurs when the customer receives the same or better experience that was promised in the company's advertising, its word-of-mouth, or any other means of communication.

Anything less than the promised experience, whether promised by advertising, marketing, or word of mouth, is the business equivalent of the kiss of death. The net result of an Authentic experience, however, is the bliss that occurs when a consumer's expectations are met or exceeded, which can lead to repeat business, positive word of mouth, and explosive growth.

It would be simple if there were a list of all the things that people regularly wanted from those with whom they do business, but not everyone has the same measuring stick.

Here Comes the Judge . . . and It's Not You

From the moment someone hears about you, decides to seek you out, and finally makes the effort to call or visit you, a set of expectations are formed about the experience. How the expectations are met becomes the basis for that customer's opinion, and how he will speak about your business in the future. Authenticity is ultimately judged by the consumer. And even though service levels are declining in nearly every major category, the customers of today are becoming more demanding than ever.

They can see through the thin veils of hype and exaggeration. They've heard and seen it all before. The customer is looking for real, honest products and services that live up to the promises made about them.

Reality Sells is both a primer and a road map for you to begin to create Authenticity in your business or workplace. It combines advertising and training to create an authentic environment in which sales and service levels can increase.

The concepts are based on the premise that you can improve your Authenticity level by carefully (and truthfully!) creating an improved advertising message, and then training your staff on how to deliver what the new message promises. We call this training concept "Selling the Inside," and it's clearly different than simply teaching your employees to smile and say "thank you." The better your staff understands the promises you have made in your advertising, the more likely they can meet or exceed the expectations of your customers.

CHAPTER 2
The Laws of Authenticity

When talking with people about Authenticity, we found it common for them to want a more detailed definition—a yardstick, something to measure themselves against to see if their idea of the concept matches up.

We found that it is not as simple as having an Authentic self that is labeled "good" or "bad." While everyone's idea of good and bad is different, we discovered that "Authentic" was neither; it is strictly in the eye of the beholder.

The movie *300*, released in March of 2007, was a big-screen epic recreation of the Frank Miller classic about the Battle of Thermopylae in 480 B.C., pitting the vastly outnumbered Greek Spartans against the tens of thousands of warriors of the Persian Empire. It was widely panned by movie critics, who called it one-dimensional, overly gory, and devoid of a plot. In its first weekend of release, however, *300* grossed an astounding $70 million, easily outpacing the $27 million of the film in second place.

How could a movie labeled "bad" by the experts have done so well? Because the critics weren't the target audience. The video-game generation fell in love with this movie from its first day of release, and started texting, blogging, and reviewing the film favorably on hundreds of opinion Web sites. The fans made *300* a hit because it was a visual feast for a group of passionate movie fans, who virally let everyone know how much they loved it.

300 was Authentic in its appeal to a certain group of people, and became extremely successful because of it. We believe that *you*, also, have the ability to appeal to an equally passionate group of customers.

In our research, we've studied dozens of businesses models, and from our study have created four universal Laws of Authenticity that we believe are critical to any business that wishes to grow and prosper. These four Laws are essential for any business if they are to find and understand their own uniqueness, make it an integral part of their marketing, and positively transfer it to those who serve their customers day in and day out.

The Four Laws of Authenticity are:

◆ The Law of Freedom

◆ The Law of Originality

◆ The Law of Transparency

◆ The Law of Repeatability

Imagine each of these four laws applied to the points of a fictitious compass. For centuries, navigators have relied on the compass to provide direction and reference, and we believe these laws can provide you with the same kind of direction and guidance within your business. You'll see very quickly how each individual Law has a direct bearing on your own business model, and the interpretation of each one can profoundly affect the way you run your company.

Let's look at each of the four laws in detail.

CHAPTER 3
Law #1: Freedom

Cast members at Walt Disney World are able to give most anything they feel is necessary to satisfy a guest. According to Dr. Tom Connellan, author of *Inside the Magic Kingdom: Seven Keys to Disney's Success*, Disney's system allows almost every employee the freedom to replace a meal for a guest, to give someone a souvenir as an apology, or getting a child a complimentary ice-cream cone to replace the one that was accidentally dropped.

As a budget line item, this freedom costs Disney far more than most companies would be willing to spend, but they have found that the positive word of mouth that each cast member brings to the situation is worth it. Mom will tell the story of the replaced ice-cream cone to dozens of people throughout her lifetime, and those people will feel a little bit better about bringing their money to the Mouse. For Disney cast members, freedom is knowing the limits of their authority.

> **The Law of Freedom** states that in order to be Authentic, one has to fully understand and be empowered in the role in which they operate.

Everyone in the organization needs to know what they can do—and how far they can go—to serve their customers. For frontline staff, this knowledge allows them to use their own judgment when making decisions about customer service or sales, and create satisfied customers without anyone else's help. Not every employee will have the ability to make every decision, but they should know where their role ends and the role of a superior begins.

If you're the owner or supervisor, your role in the Law of Freedom is to communicate each team member's limits, adjust them when necessary, and make sure you're someone who is seen as Authentic in the eyes of those who work under you. In order to pull this off strategically, you have to possess a good understanding of who you are, what your strengths are, and where your boundaries lie. We believe Mark Cuban is a great example.

Authentic Leader in Action: Mark Cuban

His critics say he is out of control, over-spoken, inappropriate, and dangerous. His occasional rants have cost him millions. His role in the NBA has been well publicized and often scrutinized. His thousands of fans see things differently, and they love to watch him. His enthusiasm is contagious, his leadership is intriguing, and his antics are entertaining. What's unusual is that Mark is not a player or a coach, he is a team owner, and yes, he has fans.

Mark Cuban is the owner of the Dallas Mavericks and is planting the seeds of change within the NBA. Cuban is not your typical team owner because he doesn't act like a team owner, and his fans love it. His fans are not the business-suit groupie types who surround many people in high places, they are the fans in the stands. He has become part of the show, enhancing the overall experience of being a Mavericks or NBA fan. Cuban brings Authenticity to the game.

Prior to Cuban, the Mavericks were a losing team. From points on the board to attendance, the Mavs were far from the top in the NBA. Sluggish ticket sales and poor on court performance created an opportunity for Mark Cuban to purchase the team in early 2000.

Measured by authenticity, Mark has an unusually high dose of freedom. He has had extraordinary success in the past and through these accomplishments, comes the experience and guts to try new ideas. Mark is also a billionaire. He got rich as a pioneer in the tech world by creating and selling *www.broadcast.com* to Yahoo!®. Guts, money, and love of the game are a winning combination. The money is not why Cuban is successful, don't misunderstand; *passion* is why he has been successful with the Mavericks. The money just allows him the freedom to try new ideas, even the big ones, faster than a less-endowed company. Countless businesses have big ideas without the money to make them happen. He has both, and the results manifest themselves in how he executes new ways to serve fans and enrich players.

Making the Mavericks the best team for which to play has been one of Cuban's goals. He beefed up coaching and training, and then went to work on the extra perks that players find rewarding. When traveling, the Mavs fly in a custom Boeing 757 with training facilities, gourmet food, and plenty of comfort. The comforts continue at home, with facilities and perks unmatched by any NBA team. When it comes to other NBA teams, Cuban treats each team to a gourmet meal after each game and locker-room luxuries similar to those with which he provides his own team. He wants the top NBA players to experience what it would be like to play for the Mavericks. The end result is a better game for the fans, the real winners.

The biggest treat for the fans is a winning team. After a decade-long slump, the Mavericks began winning games, entering the play-offs every year since 2001. It's fun to be a fan again in Dallas. Games are sold out (and have been at every home game since 2002), and the experience is better than ever from the food to the scoreboard. Cuban is highly visible at games, and is part of the courtside excitement. His connection to fans goes well beyond games through his popular blog, *www.blogmaverick.com*. Staying true to his technical background and passion for technology, Cuban faithfully shares his thoughts on the team, the NBA, and a myriad of other topics. He also uses it, along with e-mail, to collect ideas and feedback from fans. The blog is a great example of transparency. He is open about his thoughts, and he gives the fans a real look into the happenings of the organization. The fan has more knowledge of the team, and a chance to respond to Cuban, which creates a much deeper experience. It's a winning combination: a man with freedom who openly shares his thoughts.

Introducing "Reality Checks"

Throughout the text, we will be introducing exercises and thought-starters called "Reality Checks." They are designed to get you to think creatively about your particular business situation in light of the concepts we're discussing. You can choose to skip over them, but we suggest that you take the time to complete each one. The insights you receive from these will build upon each other as the text progresses.

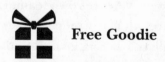 **Free Goodie**

Want a printable PDF of the Sources of Freedom? Go to the Goodie Box at *www.realitysells.com* and enter the word SOURCES in the box. Note: You will need to register if you are a first time user.

Reality Check:

Sources of Freedom

Listed are several potential sources of freedom. Consider your business in light of these sources, and rank them on a scale of one to five (five being highest) according to the level to which they enhance your current ability to do business.

Take the three highest-ranked items, and for each of them, list three ways in which each enhances your ability to do business.

My Freedom:

Education   1._____

Training   a)_____

Expertise   b)_____

Brand   c)_____

Product Line   2._____

Franchise   a)_____

Financial Strength   b)_____

Personality   c)_____

Community   3._____

Scarcity   a)_____

                      b)_____

                      c)_____

Achieving Freedom

Your freedom is what gives you permission to be original. It is a valuable asset, and just like any other asset, it can be used to benefit the business or lie dormant.

In business, understanding your freedoms and the potential advantages they give you is the first step to becoming more real. We believe that as entrepreneurs and leaders, it's important to recognize these assets as viable business strengths, and to ethically exploit them in every way you can, whether they're tangible (building, property, equipment) or intangible (your brand, knowledge, experience, etc.).

Understanding who you are, who you serve, what you serve, why you serve, and where you serve gives you the freedom to be Authentic and original.

Potential Sources of Freedom

You may understand Freedom as a concept, but the question may remain: How does it connect as a Law of Authenticity? To make this concept clear, we've listed several examples of Freedoms, and the ways in which you might consider them as assets in the discovery of your own Authenticity:

Education and Training What education do you have that gives you the skills necessary perform the work you are doing? Do you have a specialized degree that allows you to be the expert? Do you have knowledge, education, or training that adds value to your customers' experiences? Professional people all have the freedom of their education, whether formal or otherwise.

Expertise Think of expertise as mileage. It's experience that you've gained over time by reading, doing, questioning, and learning the hard way. Expertise doesn't require formal education or training; it requires hard work over an extended period of time. An expert gets paid to save someone time and money. Freedom for experts is the ability to speak and act with the authority of their working knowledge.

Brand A great brand gives you freedom to represent yourself to customers with the power of association. A brand can evoke thoughts, feelings, and opinions in customers that go beyond the shopping experience. A great brand will draw customers and help build confidence. Franchises often offer the ability to serve to customers a brand that has recognizable images, products, and feelings. Understanding your brand will allow you to better relate to customers. The freedom of having a great brand allows you to run with an established product, which allows you to spend more time on things like perfecting the service your people are providing, or sharing the brand message with new customers.

Product Line Having a good product line, and just as important, a good knowledge of that product line, allows you to have a sharper understanding of what you can do for a customer. A good line of products or services will allow you to assess the needs of the customer and present a recommended solution. If you have a weak or unattractive line, then you have to work hard to find the right customer. An overly broad product line can often make it difficult to focus on serving your ideal customer. Where does your current product line place you?

Focus Have you ever known a stupid person who became rich? Success is not directly related to intelligence. Hard work, tenacity, determination, and the ability to stay focused and stick to something are traits of very successful people. The execution of an idea is always more important than the brilliance of the thought. How sharp is your focus, and is it a freedom you enjoy today?

People The ability you have to expand, grow, and work strategically on the business is a direct result of hiring, training, and nurturing the right people for the jobs you have. With the right people in the right places, you now have a massive amount of potential freedom. Do you have this kind of freedom? And if you do, are you using it wisely?

Location Being in the right business location allows you a great deal of freedom to do many things that others in less desirable locations can only dream of. Are you using the freedom of your favorable location to its maximum advantage?

Web site In a similar way, a company's Web site is its front door to the world. The maximization of your home page, its layout, its compelling copy, and dozens of other features on your site can give you the freedom to explore other selling possibilities. The more traffic and online address captures you can successfully execute, the more you can use those addresses to create even more exciting online commerce. The freedom the World Wide Web gives businesses is just beginning to be understood. To what greater degree could you be developing your online possibilities in your quest for Authentic freedom?

There are many more potential sources of freedom that may exist in your company today. The more you can recognize them and harness their inherent power, as well as transfer that knowledge to your team, the better off you and your customers will be.

 Authenticity Point

Your sources of freedom may not be something that you wear on your sleeve. You may choose to not advertise what gives you freedom. Rather you advertise the ways you are different or unique, and why it is important to the customer. The customer may not care about your credentials, but they will care about how your credentials improve their lives. This comes from exploring originality.

 Free Goodie

Want more information and examples of freedom go to the Goodie Box at www.realitysells.com and enter the word FREEDOM in the box. Note: You will need to register if you are a first time user.

CHAPTER 4
Law #2: Originality

Ed Debevic's is a Chicago restaurant landmark that encourages its waiters and waitresses to be "sassy" with their customers. The place is covered with memorabilia from the '50s and '60s. The staff dresses up in kitsch of the era, and serves up blue-plate specials like meat loaf and chicken-fried steak, burgers and fries, and giant milk shakes. Every so often, a song comes over the sound system (played by a real, live DJ in a booth), and the entire waitstaff jumps up on the counter and does a special dance.

Every member of the team is encouraged to find and create their own original persona. The rules are that there are very few rules. Serve people originally. Find ways to connect with the guests. Help them to enjoy their visit beyond the food that's served.

Some wear dozens of campy buttons on their smock; others trade insults with the customers for fun. Some crack their gum and twirl a pencil in their hair while taking orders; others try to playfully "pick up" the dates of restaurant patrons.

Ed Debevic's is a unique combination of restaurant and theatre. People know exactly what they're going to get when they come in, and they love it. Leave the white tablecloths to someone else; Ed's is just pure, original fun.

> ✦ **The Law of Originality** states that
> you should be intensely aware of
> what makes you different, and
> celebrate it by creatively deepening that
> originality at every opportunity.

For employees, Originality is learning the rules of the road at work, and then customizing their delivery to benefit the organization, the customers, and yourself. It may mean creating a unique opening greeting to customers, wearing a distinctive item, providing the very best service in a particular category, or another original characteristic within the allowable framework of the position.

For owners and supervisors, the answer to why you're Original must start with you. Originality is knowing why you're different, determining how that brings value to your customers, and being able to transfer that knowledge to those who are on the frontline so that they can complete the circle. We think Jimmy John Liautaud is a perfect example of Originality in action.

Authentic Leader in Action: Jimmy John Liautaud

"If you were a really good customer, you'd buy more." reads the sign behind the register. On the wall, neon letters taunt, "Your mom wants you to eat at Jimmy John's." You smile, and that's the point.

As owner of a sandwich franchise that serves up fresh and fun, Jimmy John Liautaud is a true original. Starting his first shop in a garage at the age of 19, Jimmy paid his dues, developing a great menu and a fun, irreverent atmosphere that has built his self-branded network to over five hundred stores. When talking to Jimmy, you quickly realize that you are dealing with a passionate person. He is full of energy and it takes little to get him into a full-blown frenzy. Jimmy harnessed all this energy and funneled it into a brand that has its own spirited identity. His stores are filled with visual cues loaded with irreverent humor that illustrates his great products and his commitment to fun. Jimmy points out, "When you are comfortable with what you do, say it."

As a homegrown entrepreneur there are three areas that Jimmy is serious about: smart and profitable operations, high food quality, and fun. The result is a brand that can afford to be irreverent without the fear of alienating the customer base. Marketing slogans like, "The customer is usually right," "Bigger is beautifuller," and "Subs so fast you'll freak," are evident throughout their advertising and are plastered throughout the stores. His Web site (*www.jimmyjohns.com*) which features a jumping and laughing Jimmy, explains it like this:

> "At Jimmy John's we take humor seriously. One of the key ingredients of our success is the fact that our attitude is as irreverent as our sandwiches are irresistible. It's just part of who we are. You might say you can take Jimmy John's outta the campus, but you can't take the campus outta Jimmy John's. But while we might be brash and silly, we're also undeniably honest. And that's something customers can't get enough of."

Jimmy John's originality is a strategic differentiator. The message is consistent throughout the store, the advertising, and the Web site. These people seem genuine about great sandwiches, clever advertising, and making money. Ask Jimmy about the future, and he responds, "I am not worried about the future. Today, I know my bread is fresh, and I'm not out of bacon at any of my stores." His live-in-the-moment mentality has been critical in building the brand from early on.

On Jimmy's Web site are a bunch of previous ads to read or play. They all pretty much have the same message: "great food, fast." However, since they are delivered with originality, Jimmy John is able to tell his simple message over and over again in creative ways without it getting old. Creating an identity and living it loudly has created an intriguing company for Jimmy John. And intriguing companies tend to get the attention of the customer.

To truly understand Jimmy, you have to experience him in Jimmy's own words. We had the opportunity to ask him a few questions.

You personally sport a great deal of originality. What gives you your originality?

JJ: I was always last with everything I did. I was a fat kid; I was always picked last for teams. At school, I was the one people poked fun at. At home, I had a lot of responsibility at an early age. My parents loaded on the chores and really pushed me to my capacity. As a kid, I was yanked at both ends. When I became an adult, I opened a Jimmy John's with a twenty-three thousand dollar loan from my dad. I had success early on and my contemporaries didn't like me—I think they were jealous. Because I was young, the businesses people around me thought I was a little rich kid. I got comfortable going against the norm, and began to use it to my advantage. I'm not afraid to be me. And my numbers prove it. You can be original, as long as you can back it up; if you fake it, you're done.

How do you build that into your organization?

JJ: I began telling it like it is, and found it's more efficient to be brutally honest. I am lucky, I am funny, and I'm a real good accountant. I control the entire brand message, from signage, to colors, to Web site. I have an operating system that's built on total discipline and control. Consistency is built into the operations.

Have you ever been concerned that being irreverent would alienate part of your potential customer base?

JJ: No, they can go somewhere else. I don't mind offending people. I am who I am, and I am true to it. When people talk about you, it's advertising. *Free* advertising.

Was merging your own lively personality into the personality of the business a challenge?

JJ: No, everything I did was what I knew. I was all about getting the attention. I didn't have a marketing degree, but I knew that I didn't have the money to buy boring advertising. I used simple ads, with catchy words to get attention. Sometimes I run TV ads in a foreign language. It gets attention, and yet people are still able to understand the message.

What is the most important thing you have learned about customers?

JJ: Do whatever they want. Make it right. Look 'em in the eye. Under-promise and over-deliver. If you take care of customers, you don't need any coupons.

Achieving Originality

In order to achieve Authentic Originality in your business, you must first have a clear picture of who you are today and what you stand for. Not a picture of what you hope to become someday, or a wish list of what you hope people will experience when they call or come in, but a real-world view of yourself in the mirror.

 800-Pound Insight

This is NOT a "wish list" of who you want to become someday. It is an unbiased, accurate reflection of your business' good points and not-so-good points. Take a deep breath, relax, and clear your mind; this exercise will be enlightening, and could take a while to complete. Take your time. It's important information, and will put you in the right frame of mind for the remainder of the journey.

 **Free Goodie**

Want a printable PDF of What's Your Uniquely Authentic Story? Go to the Goodie Box at *www.realitysells.com* and enter the word $\boxed{\text{Unique}}$ in the box. Note: You will need to register if you are a first time user.

Reality Check:

What's Your Uniquely Authentic Story?

Business name: _____

Number of years in business: _____

Your name: _____ Number of years in the business: _____

How the business got started: _____

_____

_____

How **you** got into the business: _____

_____

_____

Why you got into the business: _____

_____

Products/Services offered: _____

_____

_____

Level of competition: _____

Competitors: _____

_____

Key benefits of doing business with you: (minimum of five)

_____

_____

_____

_____

_____

_____

Uniqueness of your business: (What makes you different?)

_____

_____

_____

_____

Current business weaknesses or soft spots: _____

_____

_____

_____

_____

Single biggest reason(s) people choose you over the competition: _____

_____

Current places your story is being told: (advertising, marketing, etc.) _____

_____

_____

_____

Main message(s) being sent to consumers about your business: (what you're telling people in your advertising)

_____

_____

Tagline or slogan used in advertising: _____

What you are most proud of about your business: _____

_____

_____

What you are least proud of: _____

_____

Plans for the future include: _____

_____

_____

Date(s) when those plans will be completed: _____

The one thing you would most like to improve right away is:

_____

_____

After completing an exercise such as this, we suggest that you give it to someone who isn't as close to the situation as you are. Give it to a spouse, a business associate, or a mentor to read. It should preferably be someone who knows your business, has experienced your product or service, and can comment on what you wrote from a first-person experience. Ask them to be brutally honest. Is it truthful? Are all the claims justifiable? Is there any exaggeration or hype? Is there anything he or she forgot to add that is significant?

Show it to a few people. Get their feedback, and make changes if appropriate.

The Painful Question

Now that you've written down your own story, answer this critical question:

If you were to close your doors today,
what would your customers miss most?

If your place were to suddenly vanish tomorrow, could your customers find another shop with similar products or services to yours relatively quickly?

Here's the reality:

You and your business are replaceable,
because what you do is probably not unique.

Think for a moment about all the places you shop and the services you use. How many of them would you rank as truly unique, the result of a great one-of-a-kind idea? And how many of them could *you* replace at a moment's notice if you had to?

When we ask most business owners and managers these questions, regardless of the number of fiercely loyal customers they think they have, most arrive at the conclusion that what they do or sell isn't so special after all. The majority of thriving businesses are built on average ideas and selling readily available products and services.

The One Thing: The Power of Differentiation

You're sick and in great pain. You make the journey to see your local physician, and after an examination, he prescribes willow bark and leaves. You are grateful for the medicine, having been fortunate to have access to one of the very best physicians around. The crude mixture, although difficult to take, gives you some relief from your pain.

The substance inside the leaves is salicin, and your doctor is the Greek physician Hippocrates. It will be 2,000 years later when chemist Felix Hoffman will synthesize salicylic acid into a stable pain-relieving powder called aspirin at the Bayer factory in Germany. By 1900, aspirin will become the number-one-selling drug worldwide.

To date, The Bayer Company has sold more than eleven billion tablets of aspirin, relieving countless aches and pains throughout its one-hundred-plus-year history. Unlike the early years, however, the three-billion-dollar analgesic industry now has many competitors.[*]

So how do companies compete in such a crowded industry with such a relatively boring product? Each of these companies has chosen to own and market a differentiator—a reason to use them. Bayer has marketed themselves as the heart-healthy aspirin-a-day company. Others claim that their formula is for headaches. Still others target sufferers of arthritis and general aches and pains.

The truth is, many of these pain relievers are fundamentally identical. While all of them may use different ingredients, they each work under the same set of medicinal principles that Felix Hoffman

---

[*]Information about The Bayer Company was obtained at
www.bayeraspirin.com/pain/asp_history.htm.

discovered over one hundred years ago. Each product, however, has taken a different twist, added or subtracted an ingredient or two, and specialized in a certain kind of pain relief. They have all created a platform that sets them apart from each other.

**What do people immediately think of
when they hear YOUR business name?**

How are you setting yourself apart within your industry? Are you as boring as a bottle of little white pills, or have you found a unique way to meet someone's need?

**The buying public should have at least
one solid reason to choose you over all
the others in your business category.**

So, let's ask the question a different way: *Why you?*

If you don't have the answer on the tip of your tongue, you cannot expect your customers—or your team members—to have it either.

So how can a business stand out from the others? Here are a few examples:

Differentiation Element:

Your Guarantee

Leon Bean was a hunter and a businessman. Born in the hills of Maine, the shoes he wore while hunting hurt his feet, so he designed a kind of waterproof, lightweight hunting boot. According to the L.L.Bean's Web site, *www.llbean.com*, Bean ordered one hundred pairs to be manufactured for sale through his family's clothing store in 1912. People raved about the new boots, and all one hundred pairs were sold; however, the thin rubber on the top part of the boot didn't hold the stitching, and ninety pairs were returned as defective.

Undaunted, Leon gave every customer that returned them a full cash refund, fixed the problem, and doubled the order from the manufacturer.

By 1919, the sideline mail-order business of selling "Maine Hunting Shoes" became so big that Leon moved his business to a larger building on the second floor of the Freeport Post Office.

Bean's "incredible guarantee" brought him legions of new customers, and the wording of his guarantee has stayed the same since it first appeared in the 1916 catalog:

> "NOTICE: I do not consider a sale complete until goods are worn out and the customer still satisfied. We will thank anyone to return goods that are not perfectly satisfactory. Should the person reading this notice know of anyone who is not satisfied with our goods, I will consider it a favor to be notified. Above all things, we wish to avoid having a dissatisfied customer."

Leon's promise redefined America's notion of customer service. Today, under the leadership of Leon's grandson, the L.L. Bean Company has nearly four thousand full-time employees and generates over $1.3 billion in sales.[†]

What's *your* guarantee to your customers? Is it in plain view for everyone to see? If you have one, do your customers know what it is? Are all of your employees aware of it? And if not, how many customers are you losing to someone else's guarantee of satisfaction?

Removing risk from a transaction by backing it completely—and making sure the customer understands your offer—is a powerful differentiator. It's also, by the way, one of the very best generators of positive word of mouth.

[†] Information obtained at
http://promomagazine.com/othertactics/marketing_satisfaction_guaranteed/index.html.

Differentiation Element:

Highest Quality

Nido Qubein, one of the greatest business speakers and consultants of our time, is a part owner of the Great Harvest Bread Company, a 210-unit chain of specialty bakeries in thirty-nine states. At an annual National Speakers Association conference, an interviewer began to ask him about how he handled competition.

"I'm sorry," he said, "but I have to stop you in the middle of your question. You see, with all due respect to you and all of the speakers in the room, I don't believe I have any competition.

"Please understand, I don't mean that as an arrogant statement on my part. Let me explain.

"I am not trying to get everyone in America to book me for speeches. I am simply trying to build solid relationships with a few people, and I know that if I deliver value to that relationship, they will tell their friends about me, and my circle will grow. So my focus, therefore, is not on what other people do, but on what I can do for others. My staff and I are constantly working on the question, 'How do we get our clients to sing our praises based on the results we deliver?' When we succeed at that, there is no competition.

"We have the same philosophy at Great Harvest Bread Company. We truly believe we have no competition. You may say, 'Nido, you're crazy! Every grocery store sells bread,' but they don't sell Great Harvest bread! No one else sells our cookies, our granola, or any of our excellent products.

"You may say, 'How can you be so sure you have no competition?' Let me tell you how I can be so sure.

"Everyone talks about brand awareness, like that's the number-one thing that business owners should capture. 'As soon as everyone knows about me, I will succeed.' That's a very erroneous and dangerous mindset, and unfortunately, it helps the local advertising media much more than the local business owner. At Great Harvest, we've developed something much deeper in the hearts and minds of our customers. We call it 'Brand Insistence.'

"People drive up to thirty miles from where they live to buy our products because they love their families and want only the best for them. We recognize that we only need a tiny fraction of the 280 million people who live in the United States to be this kind of customer for our stores, so we do everything we can to cater to that customer.

"As long as I can continue to cater to that customer, bring that customer more value, more service, and more quality products, do I really have any competition? I think not."

What is Nido really saying?

He's saying this: Great Harvest has used their overarching theme of quality products as its differentiator in the marketplace.

Where do *you* stand on quality? Is it obvious in the way you do business? Is it obvious in your cleanliness? Your products? Your employees? What could you be doing to become the quality leader in your category?[‡]

Differentiation Element:

Convenience

There are dry cleaners on every corner, but very few of them are willing to deliver to your home or workplace, seven days a week.

[‡] Information in "Differentiation Element: Highest Quality" was obtained at National Speakers Association, 2003 National Convention, New Orleans, LA, Nido Qubien: Lesson and teachings from a master.

You can buy groceries anywhere, but you can avoid the long lines and nightmarish parking by shopping at your nearest neighborhood convenience store.

People make a choice between time and money every day. Not all the reasons are logical, but your business has a convenience factor, and it's one of the factors that goes into a buying decision.

There are few logical reasons for paying seven dollars for a giant tub of buttered popcorn at the movie theatre. The convenience of having it right there as you're watching the movie, however, justifies its expense. It's convenient, you like good buttered popcorn, and it's just not the same movie experience without it.

Enterprise Rent-A-Car is the largest rental-car company in North America, with over a half million vehicles in its fleet and over five thousand offices in the United States alone. The company had always prided itself on customer service, but hit on a brilliant differentiator in 1994. That's when the company began delivering vehicles to people where they needed them, which was often at the auto body or mechanic's shop where their car was being worked on. The convenience of having a rental vehicle delivered was truly appreciated by legions of rental-car users.

"We'll Pick You Up" became Enterprise's advertising tagline, using a brown-paper-wrapped vehicle with the company's logo as its visual identifier. This single differentiator has been a key driver of Enterprise's growth, and continues to be the one thing for which the company is best known today.[§]

What makes your business convenient for others? Is it your location? Your hours? Your toll-free number or Web site? Your ordering system? Your billing practices? Your terms? Your intuitive staff members who remember what good customers order week after week?

[§] Information about Enterprise was obtained at *www.enterprise.com*.

800-Pound Insight

When consumers are given a choice between time and money, money is most often advertised, but time most often wins.

Differentiation Element:

Exclusivity/Originality

Krispy Kreme Donuts' explosive growth in the early part of the twenty-first century was fueled in part by the exclusivity of the brand. Nothing tasted quite like a Krispy Kreme, and since there weren't stores on every corner, people would drive a long way to get them.

After Krispy Kreme's rapid expansion, some of the novelty began to wear off. The company went from fewer than one hundred stores in 1998 to their products being available in over twenty thousand locations, including gas stations and grocery stores. They're still the original, but not nearly as exclusive as they once were.[**]

Callaway Golf is a premier American manufacturer of high-end golf equipment. The company's founder, Eli Callaway, is best known for creating the first wide-body, stainless-steel Big Bertha driver in the early 1990s. The new oversized clubhead was designed to be more forgiving to novice players, allowing them to hit longer, straighter drives from the tee. Golfers were quick to buy them after Mark Brooks became the first player on the PGA tour to win an

---

[**] Information about Krispy Kreme was obtained at *www.moneycentral.msn.com/content/p106124.asp.*

event using the new club in 1991. It went on to become the biggest-selling club in the history of golf.

The Big Bertha was original, it was exclusive, and its wildly new design changed the golf industry forever.[††]

Businesses have also been known to differentiate themselves by being "intravators," or those who conduct "business as usual" in unusual ways. Netflix was one of the first movie rental companies to offer its customers a way to bypass the traditional video store's draconian practices of charging late fees. The answer: Don't charge any.

Netflix's business model was one-hundred-percent online: Order what you need, we'll send it to you in a day or two, and you'll never have to pay those awful late fees. Blockbuster never saw it coming, and was soon forced to relinquish their practice of charging late fees—a half-billion-dollar annual revenue stream.

Blockbuster has since reinvented their product to compete directly with Netflix, and offers an additional benefit of having the option to send the DVDs back via the mail, or bring them back to the freestanding stores and exchange them for new ones.

Not every business has an exclusive or an original angle, but it's worth it to explore whether or not you have one that's undiscovered or unmarketed.

What are you doing that no one else is doing? What do you have that no one else has? Whom do you cater to that no one else caters to?[‡‡]

[††] Information obtained at *www.callawaygolf.com.*

[‡‡] Information about Netflix and Blockbuster obtained at: Wallstreet Journal: Netflix vs Naysayers, March 27, 2007 page E1.; *www.cheifmarketer.com/ Lazarus_blockbuster_0729-index.html; www.blockbuster.com; www.netflix.com.*

Differentiation Element:

Availability

Walgreens and CVS are two competing pharmacies that have similar goals: Make sure that wherever and whenever you need them, they won't be far away.

CVS has the most locations, with over 6,200 stores compared to Walgreens' 5,600 stores as of the end of 2006. However, Walgreens has the edge in total sales volume, with nearly $50 billion in sales in 2006 vs. $43.8 billion for CVS.[§§]

Each has its own satellite network of prescription data, so that if you're vacationing in Tampa or visiting relatives in Boise, you can obtain your prescription wherever you happen to be. Each also has an aggressive growth plan, fueled by statistics that show the sale of prescription drugs will double in the U.S. by 2012.

They don't stock each category very deeply, but they do have a wide variety of the essentials of everyday living. Whether it's tooth-picks, a curling iron, or a bag of snacks, you're likely to find what you're looking for at either CVS or Walgreens. If you need a ream of copy paper, for example, they might stock a single choice instead of the eight to ten choices you might find at an office-supply store. The good news is that they've got a ream of copy paper if you need it.

Walgreens and CVS are dedicated to making the essentials more available to the public in more places than ever before.

[§§] Information obtained at *www.finance.yahoo.com*, March 17, 2007.

Sometimes the limited availability of a product can lead to positive results.

Toyota's Scion xA and xB automobiles were an immediate hit when they were introduced in early 2004. The boxy, edgy subcompact cars were designed to appeal to younger consumers who enjoyed expressing their individuality through the vehicle they choose to drive.

Despite the demand, Toyota deliberately held back production of these cars to one hundred thousand in the first year, and one hundred fifty thousand in the second and third years. Toyota's strategy was to build value in each vehicle by making sure the vehicles remained an exclusive item to own. If there were too many of them running around, they wouldn't be as cool.***

Whether you choose the increased-availability model or the limited-availability model, ask yourself: How available is my product, and is it an asset? Does it differentiate me from others in the market? And how can I ethically exploit the availability aspect of what I sell or do?

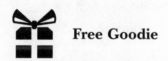 **Free Goodie**

Want a printable PDF of the Differentiators list? Go to the Goodie Box at *www.realitysells.com* and enter the word DIFFERENTIATOR in the box. Note: You will need to register if you are a first time user.

*** Information about Toyota's strategy obtained at
http://online.wsj.com/article_print/SB116313070935919553.html.

Reality Check:

Differentiators – A List

Use this thought-starter to compile a list of brand differentiators you currently possess, and a separate list of differentiators that you'd like to develop and be known for in the future:

		Currently Have:	Want in the Future:
Products:	Variety of Merchandise	___	___
	Quality (Value-Priced, Mid-Grade, Premium)	___	___
	Brands Available	___	___
	Latest Fashions/Technology/ Cutting Edge Trends	___	___
	Availability (In Stock)	___	___
	Guarantees/Warranties	___	___
	Delivery	___	___
	Return Policy	___	___
	Nationally Advertised (Well-Known)	___	___
	Other: _____	___	___
	_____	___	___
	_____	___	___
Services:	Variety of Services Performed	___	___
	Experience	___	___
	Expertise	___	___
	Specialization	___	___

Technicians/Personnel   ____   ____

Education/Training   ____   ____

Guarantees/Warranties   ____   ____

Proper Licensing/Bonding   ____   ____

Equipment Used   ____   ____

On-Time Record   ____   ____

Nationally Advertised
(well-known)   ____   ____

Locally Owned & Operated   ____   ____

Other: _____   ____   ____

_____   ____   ____

_____   ____   ____

Pricing: Aggressive, Low-Price Leader   ____   ____

Premium-Priced (Value-
Based)   ____   ____

Other: _____   ____   ____

Locations: Convenience   ____   ____

Multiple Locations   ____   ____

Size of Locations (Small or
Large)   ____   ____

New Locations   ____   ____

Parking   ____   ____

Other: _____   ____   ____

Personnel: Talented Face-to-Face Service
Providers   ____   ____

Talented Service Providers on
the Telephone   ____   ____

Well-Educated on
Products/Services   ____   ____

	Provide "Value-Added" Experiences to Customers	___	___
Hours:	Longer Hours	___	___
	24-7 Service	___	___
	Weekend Hours	___	___
	Evening Hours	___	___
	Other: _____	___	___
Specials:	Special Events	___	___
	Special Sales	___	___
	Frequent-Shoppers Club/Discounts	___	___
	Incentives for Repeat Business	___	___
Marketing:	Brand Identity	___	___
Intangibles:	Reputation (Local, Regional, National, Worldwide)	___	___
	Business Image	___	___
	Store "Feel"	___	___
	Positive Word-of-Mouth Endorsements/Testimonials from Others	___	___
	Other: _____	___	___
	_____	___	___

How to Use this Newfound Originality

Now that you've found your differentiators, how do you share them with the world?

The differentiators you establish become the basis upon which you will begin to communicate everything about your business. Originality is what you do that improves the life of the customer that no one else can do quite like you.

 Free Goodie

Want more information and examples of originality go to the Goodie Box at *www.realitysells.com* and enter the word ORIGINALITY in the box. Note: You will need to register if you are a first time user.

CHAPTER 5
Law #3: Transparency

Transparency is a complicated word. It can mean "open, frank, or candid," and "easily seen-through, recognized, or detected."

Would you call advertising an open, frank, and candid form of communication? Most advertising sounds so hyped-up and non-genuine that it tends to get dismissed as too slick.

In an Authentic environment, customers are looking for you to be open, frank, and candid with them in every way. And when you're not, they can easily dismiss you as phony or fake, and be less inclined to trust you.

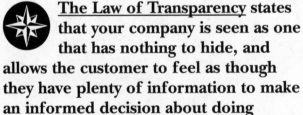

> **The Law of Transparency** states **that your company is seen as one that has nothing to hide, and** allows the customer to feel as though they have plenty of information to make an informed decision about doing business with you.

Transparency is one of those elements that must start from the top. It begins as a story, and includes an open, honest look at how the Freedom and Originality of the business affect the life of the customer.

Transparency is how you share what you do in a way that isn't hyped, overblown, or phony. Transparency means that every person on the staff is "in the know" about what's going on, including current advertising, product offerings, and benefits to potential customers. They also know what their offerings *can't* do for people, and are honest enough to steer people in the right direction when they don't have the solution.

The long-term result of Transparency is trust. When customers see you as precisely who you are, you give them the ultimate tool with which to choose whether or not to do business with you. We believe Roy H. Williams not only embodies Freedom and Originality, but he also does an excellent job of being Transparent.

Authentic Leader in Action: Roy H. Williams

Combine one part each of perception and curiosity, sprinkle with originality and freedom, and shake well. Place in a quiet room until done. It may take a few days, or a week or two to emerge. When done, be prepared to be entertained, taught, exposed, shared with, and given to. Meet Roy H. Williams, the self-proclaimed Wizard of Ads, Chancellor of Wizard Academy, a school for communication arts in the hill country of Texas, and best-selling author of several books including the *Wizard of Ads* trilogy.

Through his weekly e-mail, *www.mondaymorningmemo.com,* Williams shares stories and insights into business, life, religion, advertising, and happiness. His memo is read by thousands and is a portal into his thoughts, concerns, beliefs, and dreams. Williams is authentic, and has earned freedom through a life of research, thinking, writing, and sharing the result of his thoughts. We accept his musings because he is the Wizard. When asked, "What's with the name 'Wizard Academy'? Are you guys a cult, or what?"

Williams answers with a sigh:

"We get asked that question a lot.

"No, we don't have anything to do with witches, warlocks, séances, Harry Potter, or Halloween. Any student of language will tell you that 'wizard' simply means 'wise man.'

"A person who cowers is a coward. A person always drunk is a drunkard. A person who is dull is a dullard. A person who is wise is a wisard. Since the "s" is pronounced as a 'z,' it came to be spelled with a 'z.'

"The person who gathers and catalogs information so that he or she might be able to give good advice at critical times is a wise-ard, or wizard. The insights he provides might seem like magic, but they're merely the result of careful investigation fueled by curiosity."[†††]

His self-proclamation of Wizard gives him the freedom to write about topics like passion, the constructs of a good ad, and success. As readers we accept a wide variety of stories from the Wizard. If they were just from Roy, he would be seen as an eccentric Texan. His freedom comes from the branding all the knowledge he has gained from studying humanity and communication into the wise man.

Williams has become recognized as one of advertising relevant experts because of his constant questioning, and watching what works. In a "Monday Morning Memo" titled "The Future of Ad Writing," he shares some insight:

"America has been flattered by advertising ("Because you deserve it!"), misled by ads ("Lowest prices anywhere!"), hyped by ads ("While supplies last"), and lied to repeatedly ("Guaranteed!"). The result of all this misinformation is a growing numbness to ad-speak. We're becoming deaf and blind to it. With effortless ease, we shut it out of our minds.

"Why are advertisers happy when their ads sound like ads?

[†††] Information about Wizard Academy was obtained at *www.wizardacademy.com.*

"Once-effective phrases become clichés when overused. Remember the '70s? Guys with long, pointed collars and blow-dried hair used the standard pick-up line, 'Do you come here often?' They did it because it worked. They quit only when the ladies began laughing at them.

"But advertising still wears that ridiculous collar and blow-dried hair because its rejection was never face-to-face. We don't laugh at ads. We quietly ignore them.

"When demand is high and supply is low, your ads need only tell the world, 'We've got it!' But how often do you actually get to do this?

Advertising—when you're building a brand—is merely a relationship deepener. Its job is to cause the public to like you and trust you. Accomplish this, and they'll remember you when they, or any of their circle, need what you sell."[‡‡‡]

Williams' ability to measure the pulse of America is the foundation for what he says about advertising. His lens is in focus, and the result is often a vivid description of what he has picked up on. Equal to his skills of observation is his ability to share his conclusions in vivid ways. In one of his weekly memos, Williams talks about how things are changing in reality TV.

"Do you remember when America watched awards shows?

"If you were somehow unplugged and didn't receive the newsflash, the combined strength of Paul McCartney, Madonna, U2, Mariah Carey, Coldplay, Faith Hill, and Jay-Z wasn't enough to swing the hammer and ring the bell during [the 2006] *Grammy Awards*. A frail 17 million watched these legends read their cue cards, while a muscular 28.3 million

---

[‡‡‡] Information about "Monday Morning Memo" was obtained at *www.mondaymorningmemo.com*—Jan. 23, 2006.

cheered hopeful, nameless kids singing their hearts out on *American Idol.*

"It was just one more indication of how we're moving away from the vertical hero-worship of Idealism to establish the horizontal links that mark an emerging Civic generation. . . .

"Unfiltered authenticity is the new cool. And volunteerism is on the rise."§§§

Anyone skeptical of a man called a Wizard need only spend a few moments reading a few memos, or leafing through a few pages from his books to be drawn to understand the depth and openness of the man behind them. He uses transparency to paint a real picture of himself—and his business. He shares his knowledge openly, sharing brilliant advertising tips without compensation.

Avoiding Ad-Speak

"Contrary to popular belief, Americans don't hate advertising.

"We just hate ads that sound like ads.

"Do your ads sound like ads? Are you guilty of ad-speak?

"Ad-speak is filled with polished words and filtered phrases that deliver no information and have no relevance. Ambiguous claims give ad-speak a hollow sound.

"Do your ads mention your superior service, your friendly staff, or name the number of years you've been in business?

"Let me know how that works out for you.

---

§§§ Information about "Monday Morning Memo" was obtained at *www. mondaymorningmemo.com*—Feb. 20, 2006.

"A meaningless statement remains meaningless no matter how often it's heard. Repetition has become a blunt instrument. Top of Mind Awareness isn't enough anymore. Today's customer expects meaningful information and lots of details."[****]

Achieving Transparency

While there are hundreds of ways you might achieve this sort of trust, we believe there are four elements to achieving transparency in business: openly sharing expertise, embracing the negatives, talking about what you don't do, and giving the customer enough information to feel like an insider.

Openly Sharing Expertise

In our minds, Roy Williams exemplifies the use of sharing expertise to achieve transparency. Within the generous amount of content he provides, Williams gently reminds his readers that he is the Wizard, and when you have a need for marketing support, who better than the expert to meet your needs?

One of his greatest gifts is being able to tell a story about someone, yet his audience ends up believing the story is about them. While others are more guarded about who they are and what they stand for, Roy is an example of someone who is very open about who he is and what he does.

Embracing the Negatives

White Castle hamburgers are known to many as "Sliders." There are several theories and wives' tales about why they're called

---

[****] Information about "Monday Morning Memo" was obtained at *www.mondaymorningmemo.com*—Aug. 28, 2006.

Sliders; one of them is that they slide easily down the hatch because of their size.

"We're not quite sure who actually came up with that name," says Jamie Richardson, White Castle's Director of Marketing. "Some of it is regional. In St. Louis, they've been known as 'Belly Bombers.' We believe it has something to do with the temptation to have more than one, but we leave the interpretation up to our customers."

For a long time, White Castle suppressed the Sliders nickname, but today they recognize its value, putting it on some of their signage and point-of-purchase materials. "Slyders®" (as it's now spelled and trademarked) are uniquely White Castle, and their corporate office has now recognized the value of promoting that differentiator.

"A lot of people here in the corporate office didn't like the negative connotation, but we saw that the name was consumer-driven, so rather than fight it, we decided to embrace it," says Richardson. "We're willing to be a little self-deprecating to better differentiate ourselves in the marketplace."

They were also smart enough to recognize that their product would never appeal to everyone. "We've known since we began that the taste of a little burger with onions can be polarizing; you either like them or you don't. Those who love and enjoy the product—and we have lots of them—consider the word 'Slyders®' a term of endearment."

Indeed, the little square hamburger even has a White Castle Hall of Fame in their home town of Columbus, Ohio, where people nominate themselves or someone else for induction.

Richardson was there at the first Hall of Fame induction in 2001. "We were a little nervous. We thought we'd get maybe fifteen or twenty entries if we were lucky." They wound up with over fifteen hundred entries, many of them multipage novels about their lives and what White Castle means to them.

You might get a little square hamburger somewhere else, but people are nuts about the little White Castle hamburgers, and they sell over five hundred million of them every year.

 800-Pound Insight

Back in my college days in the early '80s, when my friends and I had the late-night munchies, we would travel forty five miles one way on I-65 from Rensselaer, Indiana to the White Castle on Route 30 in Merrillville. In our minds, nothing else would quite satisfy like a sackful of those little square burgers at 2:00 a.m. Do your customers go out of their way to do business with you like that?

Talk About What You Don't Do

For years, spokesperson Tom Bodett let us know about all the things that you won't get at a Motel 6 compared to the big hotel chains. Today, riding on the success of that long-running ad campaign, Motel 6 is one of the most successful lodging companies of the past twenty-five years. It was successful because Motel 6 wasn't afraid to let people know what they weren't, which was fancy and expensive. Obviously, the Authentic ad campaign worked, and the rest is history.

 800-Pound Insight

A new furniture store opened up in the small community of Bradley, Illinois. The new owner's concept was to sell name-brand furniture at discount prices out of a no-frills warehouse, but he wasn't sure how to advertise it. He came to me as a long-time friend and asked for my help.

"I don't want to be like everyone else, Bill," he said. "But I don't know how to advertise any other way than 'SALE, SALE, SALE.' It's a drug I don't want to have to use every week to drive traffic into my store."

In looking at his operation, I was impressed. He had obviously thought through the concept very well. His furniture was indeed excellent quality by well-known names in the industry, and it was well displayed in neat rows, on a freshly painted cement floor in a sparse but clean warehouse.

When it came time to promote his store, I decided to write ads that focused on the things he didn't have versus what he did have. We used his voice on the radio ads, and talked about his no-frills warehouse as a less-expensive way to buy quality furniture.

"We don't have a fancy showroom, sophisticated displays, or carpeting to help you visualize what your new furniture will look like in your home," the ads said, "but if you've got a little imagination and don't mind saving a lot of money, Furniture Brands Outlet is the perfect place for you."

His first year in business blew away all of his expectations, and today he's talking about expansion into other markets.

Give the Customer Enough Information to Feel Like an Insider

Carnival Cruise Lines is one of the largest vacation companies in the world, with twelve different cruise-line brands in its portfolio, including Princess, Holland America, Cunard, Windstar, Costa, and P&O.

Carnival markets themselves to people who are new to cruising in various traditional media. But if you are a past cruise traveler, you become special. Carnival markets the past cruisers much more heavily, promoting the cruise experience via e-mail, postcards, and enticing catalogues detailing destinations and locales that have been preselected through past guest questionnaires. The beautiful magazines and postcards do their job of whetting your appetite, and the special offers that are made via e-mail for special last-minute getaways and cabin-upgrade offers "limited ONLY to past guests" make the recipients feel like they're in on something that the rest of the world just doesn't receive.

 800-Pound Insight:

How do I know about all this Carnival information? Because I get it all at home! My family and I recently enjoyed a Carnival cruise ourselves, and I've noticed the masterful marketing they create to try to get me back. It's working.

What Carnival does exceptionally well is to make past cruisers feel like they're in on something that no one else gets to know, i.e., "You're special because you know what it's like on one of our cruises, you're one of the family."

At Swarovski Crystal Worlds near Innsbruck, Austria, visitors come from all over the world to see the magnificent Chambers of Wonder, garden and displays created by the makers of the "world leader in precision-cut crystal."

Originally constructed in 1995 in honor of the 100th anniversary of the company, the multi-faceted subterranean attraction is a Mecca to the art and fascination of crystal. Conceived and created by avant-garde international media artist Andre Heller, visitors are greeted by the Giant of Wattens, an enormous garden fountain formed from the mountainside in the shape of a giant's head, with huge sparkling eyes made of Swarovski crystal and water spouting from its mouth.

Each of the many Chambers of Wonder inside the museum are a kind of living kaleidoscope of breathtaking displays, weaving crystal creations using inspiration and art from Andy Warhol, sculpture from Salvador Dali and Niki de Saint Phalle, photography by Giselle Freund and Edward Steichens, and many others. Tourism companies describe it as "a three-dimensional adventure museum", and according to Swarovski, Crystal Worlds hosts more than 700,000 visitors a year.

After the museum tour, you're escorted into the gift shop, where a "one-of-a-kind shopping experience" awaits Swarovski fans. All the newest pieces are available for sale, displayed in breathtaking grandeur. At this point, visitors have an extremely high sense of value for these pieces, and they sell like hot cakes.

If you're a member of the International Swarovski Crystal Society, a collector's club, you receive extra-special treatment at Crystal Worlds, including admittance to a VIP lounge, a glass of champagne upon arrival, and an exclusive showroom of items reserved only for Society members. Value, value, value. It is retail theatre at its finest.

The transparent experience allows Swarovski to add significant value to their product, as well as an emotional bond with their visitors that transcends everything. When you've been to the Crystal Worlds in Austria, there is no competition.

Transparency in Advertising: It's All About the Customer

Historically, the advertising industry is not one that boasts its Authenticity. There are, however, very effective ways in which advertising is being used today to promote customer benefits instead of bragging about the merits of the company.

One way to become more Authentic in your advertising is to ask the question "So what?" to each statement you make regarding your business. Take a moment right now and come up with a fact about your business about which you're particularly proud. State that fact out loud. Then pretend you're a customer, and ask the question, "So what?" Answer why it is important from the customer's perspective. Then ask again, "So what?" Answer it again. Keep asking the question, "So what?" until the essence of the benefit comes out.

For example, a tire-repair shop might make the following statement:

"We have six technicians waiting to serve you."

What would a potential customer think after hearing this statement?

"Is six good or bad?"
"Six people to fix a tire? I'll bet they're expensive."
"If they are just waiting, they must not be all that busy."
"Technicians? Do they all need to be technicians to change a tire?"
Okay, let's ask the question: "So what?"
"We have six technicians waiting to serve you."   So what?
"So you don't have to wait."   So what?
"So you don't have to put off fixing the tire."   So what?
"So your family will be safer with a repaired tire."
Ah! Finally, the nugget worth talking about! Family safety!
Here's our new ad, written with the benefit to the customer in mind:

At Speedy Tire, we know that safety is your number-one concern, and when it comes to your vehicle, having safe tires and a spare tire that is ready to go is smart. When the unexpected happens to your tires, our six Speedy Tire technicians will make sure you get the service you need as quickly as possible, and check for potential trouble spots on your other tires. You see, at Speedy Tire we believe you shouldn't have to decide between your family's safety and your busy schedule.

If you have a tire issue and are near Speedy Tire, are you going to put off fixing it? Probably not. If Speedy Tire gets the job done right and you only have to wait a short amount of time to have it fixed, will you be willing to pay five dollars more than the cheapest place in town? Yes, because you believe Speedy Tire cares about your schedule and your safety.

Tell them what they will love most about you. Avoid telling them what *you* love most about you. Just for the heck of it, count the number of "you"s and "your"s in that Speedy Tire ad, and then count the number of "we"s. There should always be more you's than we's and I's.

Here's another example: You might think that your coffee is a best seller because of the Columbian beans that are only picked on the east side of the mountain on Tuesday. If someone asked twenty five of your best customers, you might find that it's a best seller because your location is the only place to get a cup of coffee between where they live and the interstate.

Your story is the beans. Your customers' story is the convenience.

Most advertisers like to brag about themselves in their ads, instead of explaining how their product or service can improve customers' lives. Maybe some of these examples sound familiar:

◆ We've been in business since 1945.

◆ We have a friendly, professional staff.

◆ We have beautiful delivery trucks.

◆ We've just invested in new display racks.

◆ We won't be undersold.

◆ We

◆ We

◆ We

◆ We

Remember who cried "We, we, we, we"? That's what the fifth Little Piggy said, who cried all the way home . . . probably because all he was thinking about was himself.

If you talk to people about you, nobody cares. If you talk to people about them, they'll listen.

 **Free Goodie**

Want more information and examples of transparency go to the Goodie Box at *www.realitysells.com* and enter the word TRANSPARENCY in the box. Note: You will need to register if you are a first time user.

CHAPTER 6
Law #4: Repeatability

A single experience does not create Authenticity; the repeated, multiple applications of that experience over time create Authenticity. The franchise model works well for creating the systems and standards for operations, but only if the execution works well at the street level of all locations. Operations are operations, and regardless of who is completing the task, the task should be done right. Personality, on the other hand, can be either engaging or indifferent. And indifference is the last emotion we want any customer to feel.

> **The Law of Repeatability** states that you have to be consistent in your products, communication, and service to customers. Your Authentic business should be able to serve everyone equally well, regardless of who's doing the serving.

Authentic Leadership in Action: The Cathy Family

In 1946, Truett Cathy—founder and CEO of Chick-fil-A, Inc.—began his restaurant career by opening The Dwarf Grill in Hapeville,

Georgia, a suburb of Atlanta. Twenty-one years later, Truett launched the start of the chain by opening the first Chick-fil-A® location at the Greenbriar Shopping Center. He kept his focus on operations and created a business model that has grown steadily over the years. His family eventually joined the management team, with sons Dan and Don earning key leadership roles. The Chick-fil-A business has grown to over thirteen hundred locations in thirty-seven states and over two billion dollars a year in sales. His business is one of the largest privately owned restaurant chains in the world. His advertising is famous, his service is exceptional, and his principles are at the forefront.

Truett, believes in doing the very best. "It is when we stop doing our best work that our enthusiasm for the job wanes. We must motivate ourselves to do our very best, and by our example lead others to do their best as well." To have a successful franchise the business has to be built on standards. How the standards are lived out often determines the success of the company. Chick-fil-A, operates under the simple mission, *"Be America's best quick-service restaurant."*

Strong business leaders have been told to lead with their hearts; this company leads with its soul. The company's Web site, *www.chick-fil-a.com* puts it this way:

The Corporate Purpose states: **"To glorify God by being a faithful steward of all that is entrusted to us and to have a positive influence on all who come in contact with Chick-fil-A."**

"That's why we invest in scholarships, character-building programs for kids, foster homes and other community services. Come to think of it, it's also not a bad motive for striving to serve a really, really good chicken sandwich."

These folks believe in what they do, and back it up with actions. They started with three simple rules: **Listen** to the customer; Focus on getting **better** before trying to get bigger; Emphasis on **quality**. The plan has worked brilliantly as they have realized sales growth for thirty-nine straight years. As the business has grown so has their commitment to their mission. Chick-fil-A restaurants have always been closed on Sundays. Truett Cathy created a foundation that operates foster-care homes that care for over one hundred thirty children, and the company supports countless charities. The chain provides educational scholarships for its restaurant employees with no strings attached. They have been able to attract a very loyal following because they execute brilliantly. Visit a store, and you will likely hear what has become a trademark phrase, "It's my pleasure." They have received industry awards for service year after year.

Part of the company's recent success has been due to an unbelievably successful marketing campaign featuring the Chick-fil-A "Eat Mor Chikin®" Cows. The Cows are featured on billboards, painting signs with funny misspelled sayings like, "Eat Mor Chikin" and "Take a Vacashun Frum Beef." The Cows have grown into plush toys and calendars, and are a key part of the corporate brand image. With great operations, sound values, incredible branding, and huge success what is quite amazing is the connection to the customer.

When a new restaurant opens, the first one hundred customers get one free combo meal per week for an entire year. People flock to the restaurant the day before to be one of the first in line. The parking lot turns into a camp out, where sometimes Cows make appearances, and samples of food are offered. It is an event fitting of the company's culture. Oftentimes Dan Cathy, who serves as president, is there to make some opening remarks, share the mission of the company, and spend time with customers. He loves being at the parties and when things wind down, and people begin to turn in, he is known to pitch a tent and sleep in the parking lot. He does this dozens of times per year. You can always tell the difference between involved and committed: Go, Dan!

Franchises work hard to create a formula that can be duplicated wherever a location is placed. The system is put together so that those who build the location according to the plans, read the manual, attend the training, and follow the steps will reap the benefits right away instead of learning things the hard way.

In a franchise, everyone makes the product in exactly the same way. A sandwich in any franchised fast-food joint should be made to the same specifications at 11:00 a.m. as it is at 7:00 p.m., and should be prepared the same way on the East Coast as it is on the West Coast. The expectation of the customer is that the sandwich they bought in Boston last week will be the same as the one they're buying in San Diego today.

Likewise, in a single hardware store, a customer should be able to expect with a reasonable degree of certainty that he will be treated the same way each time he shops. It doesn't matter if Ed, the plumbing expert, isn't there today; someone else should be able to pick up the slack and help the customer with plumbing questions on any given day. Everyone's using the same playbook.

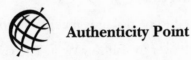 **Authenticity Point**

Throughout my years in the restaurant business, one of the most valuable lessons I learned was in my hiring. I would hire people who fit the skills of the job, and put up with the personality issues that arose. Sometimes it took me too long to get rid of someone who really didn't fit. After several hires that were marginal at best, I began to interview with personality in mind. My only interest in their past experience was learning how they described their job and where they worked. I learned to dig for the personality, and make decisions based on people who had a spark to them. It sometimes took longer to find someone, but in the long run, it paid off. Hire for attitude; train for skills.

Achieving Repeatability

Chick-Fil-A would not be nearly as successful if the entire staff wasn't one-hundred-percent on board with Truett Cathy's vision of service. It's important, therefore, to make sure that the actions that are repeated are the right actions.

Give Value First: A Tale of Two Cities

Jack is a tour-bus driver in Key West, Florida. His job is to take cruise-ship passengers back and forth from the port of Key West to the popular shopping and dining areas of the island town in his trolley-like open-air vehicle.

Jack has another job. And frankly, he stinks at it.

Jack's "other" job is supposed to take place while he's performing his real job. Both jobs should happen simultaneously, but in Jack's world, that's not the case.

What Jack is supposed to be doing is making visitors smile.

People come from all over to visit Key West. The visions of Jimmy Buffett, lazy warm days, a carefree escape from the real world . . . it's all there.

But the sunny hospitality doesn't start with Jack.

Somewhere along the way, Jack got old and crusty. At some point in his driving career, he decided that talking with passengers was too much work. Instead, he started talking AT them.

He began asking for tips over the loudspeaker. Then he started asking for them earlier and earlier into the trip through Key West. Now, Jack asks for tips three times during every load of passengers he takes. And barely anyone gives him the time of day, much less their spare change.

What poor Jack has forgotten is the golden rule of a successful business:

GIVE VALUE FIRST.

Before you ask for anything of value, you must first prove yourself value-worthy to your customer. And that sometimes means doing something nice for someone without expecting anything at all in return.

Isaac is a value-giver. And Isaac is much richer than his friend Jack.

Isaac is a tour guide in Cozumel, Mexico, a beautiful cruise-ship destination that has many shore excursions. Isaac is employed by a company that runs bus excursions to an exclusive Cozumel beach area called Passion Island.

Throughout the twenty-minute bus trip, Isaac delightfully describes the surrounding jungle areas to his passengers in a fun, interesting way over the loudspeaker. He talks to several of the passengers, gets to know their names, and asks where they're from.

The last five minutes of the bus ride is the bumpiest, most treacherous road on which anyone on the trip has ever traveled. Because of the wildlife-refuge status of the area, the road is not allowed to be repaired, and so it must remain in this condition. It could potentially be an awful experience for those on the bus, but Isaac tells them it's their "Mexican massage," and that it's free for all the passengers today. Everyone laughs and enjoys the bumpy ride.

Isaac is personal, enjoyable, and real.

"I've been doing this work for several years, and it never gets old," Isaac says. "People come up to me all the time and say, 'Hi, Isaac! My friend from Buffalo said to come and see you. She was here about six months ago. Her name is Joy, she was about five-foot, nine-inches tall . . .' There's no way I would remember her, but people are comfortable enough to come and talk to me like I'm a friend of the family."

But what's the one thing that makes Isaac different from Jack?

"My wife tells me, 'Isaac, you're not just going to a job. You're doing something you love, and you do it for the people, not yourself.' I believe that's the secret. Love what you do, and do it for the sake of others. That, in turn, will bring your reward."

If Jack ever had the secret to start with, he lost it long ago.

Isaac gives value first. He does his very best for the sake of others, without any expectations.

And get this: He never asks for tips, but gets far more money in tips from those on his tours than anyone else.

Are you old and crusty like Jack? Or alive and giving of yourself like Isaac? How much value do you deliver to others without asking for anything in return?

Simply repeating an action over and over is not necessarily the right way. Jack's actions are being repeated in the WRONG way.

To be able to repeat the same excellence over and over again, we believe that it's important to look at the three main phases of the customer experience:

- **The Preconceived Notion** — Before the Experience
  This is the sum total of everything a consumer is exposed to about your business prior to their first encounter with you. This includes everything from delivery trucks, banners, radio ads, and Little League sponsorships to the word of mouth that happens at the corner coffee shop. It could be positive, negative, somewhere in between, or nonexistent.

- **The Moment of Truth** — During the Experience
  Your customer has a need for what you do, and has decided to call or visit. At that moment, your customer has an expectation of what is about to happen based on that preconceived notion. Judgments are being made every second on the quality of the experience. Everything must come together at this moment. If there's a difference between the expected experience and the actual experience, it needs to be on the plus side.

- **The Ongoing Impression** — After the Experience
  How your customer feels about the Moment of Truth will dictate the customer's future behavior, as well as color their

thoughts and actions regarding your product or service in the future. Future word of mouth, repeat business, and even the desire for the product or service you provide all spin off of this ongoing impression. More important, these impressions can last for a very long time.

 800-Pound Insight

Have you ever held onto an impression of a business for more than a year? Longer? A lot can change in a year's time, yet your impression remains. It's something to remember when you're considering the importance of the Moment of Truth and its effect on the Ongoing Impression.

As you can see, most everything falls on the Moment of Truth to move the relationship forward. How you treat people at that moment will determine the present and future value of the relationship.

Every entrepreneur believes they have that special something to offer that will bring them success in business. The problem is that there's an overabundance of confident business owners who truly believe they have the right idea.

We believe that scores of small businesses fail because too many people have the "Right Idea."

It's not that the ideas are bad. On the contrary, many small-business ideas are genuinely innovative or creative adaptations of someone else's successful concept. They lack the proper planning and execution of the idea at the customer level. Ideas must be followed through completely, and given the proper foundation to succeed.

Entrepreneurs are often in danger of falling in love with their idea or concept too deeply. They think it's great, assume others will think it's great too, and forge ahead. "Build it and they will come" worked in the movie *Field of Dreams*, but not in the business world.

There is a sobering reality to understand:

**Most new businesses
are just another opportunity
to buy an already-available
product or service.**

As an entrepreneur, it's difficult to admit this. Even though you may have a new spin on an old idea, most everything's already out there being sold. Yet somehow, enough of these average businesses selling ordinary products seem to produce reasonable wealth for their owners. Ordinary stuff sold to ordinary people. That's how most businesses operate.

So if most of the stuff is just a commodity, how is it that some businesses do it so much more successfully than others?

It's fairly simple:

**Successful businesses
control the customer experience
better than the competition.**

What do we mean when we talk about the customer experience? Is it the parking lot? Their contact on the telephone? The employees' appearance? The inside temperature of the store? The packaging?

The answer is YES. And it's far more than just these factors.

If you don't control the environment when the customer is on the phone or in your store, you've lost the most important link in the food chain. And we mean that literally. Without a great customer experience, your food chain will be broken.

But unfortunately, not everyone in business keeps their promises.

**According to a study by the customer
experience group Beyond Philosophy,
eighty percent of customers said
their experiences don't match**

**the promises made in brand communications,
and more than eighty percent of them are disappointed.**[††††]

That means that four out of five consumers believe that a product's advertising *misled* them in their decision to buy.

No wonder people are so jaded by advertising!

So how will your staff know what it is you're telling consumers in their ads? Welcome to "Selling the Inside."

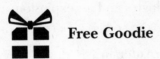 **Free Goodie**

Want more information and examples of repeatability go to the Goodie Box at *www.realitysells.com* and enter the word REPEATABILITY in the box. Note: You will need to register if you are a first time user.

Selling the Inside™
Twelve Reasons to Embrace It

If your advertising is strong enough to bring people to your door, the service they receive is one of the strongest variables as to whether or not they'll return. We believe that one of the key reasons that employees seem disengaged, uninterested, and lazy is because they haven't been given a reason to feel or to be otherwise.

Selling the Inside is a more comprehensive way of looking at training. It's a holistic approach that allows each team member to fully understand his employer's mission, values, and philosophy, in addition to what, how, and why the company is advertising, and how all of the above affects him. More importantly, it allows him to see how each one affects all of the above as an individual contributor to the overall success of the organization.

[††††] Information obtained at *www.crmguru.com/editor/top_10/1677.php*.

Selling the Inside is a philosophy that extends beyond the concept of traditional training. You may already be doing parts of it, but it's unlikely that you're doing all of it.

If you're trying to achieve authenticity, here is why we believe **Selling the Inside** is one of its most important components.

1. Advertising is expensive.

The cost of getting the word out has never been higher. Even with the advent of new technologies and an explosion of new advertising and marketing companies, the cost to advertise is rising sharply.

Weekday newspaper readership is down over fifteen percent since 1990, slipping by over six percent in a single twelve-month period between March 2005 and March 2006.[‡‡‡‡] Despite their eroding numbers, any advertiser will tell you that newspaper-advertising rates continue to increase each year. Radio has diluted their impact by adding thousands of station choices since 1970, yet their average rates have also increased substantially during that time. Television viewers were limited to a handful of over-the-air stations a generation ago, but now with cable, satellite, and computer hookups for programming, TV watchers are scattered among hundreds of niche channels. There is no such thing as "mass media" any longer.

To make matters worse, the proliferation of advertising is decreasing its overall effectiveness. A recent poll by Emergence, an Atlanta-based brand-consulting firm, found that consumers are turning a deaf ear to the taglines that brands use to define themselves. Over 500 people were tested for their recall of taglines for twenty-five of America's best-known companies. While sixty-seven percent associated "Always low prices. Always." with Wal-Mart, second-place Sprite scored just thirty-five-percent recognition for "Obey your thirst." Thirteen of the twenty-five slogans tested scored

---

[‡‡‡‡]Information obtained at *www.naa.org/info/facts04/readership-audience.html* and *www.rab.com/public/media/detail.cfm* on March 2007.

single-digit recognition among the more than five hundred consumers interviewed.*

Knowing all this, a business still must invest in advertising. You can't throw a party and not send out invitations. But there is a way that business owners can make their ad dollars work more efficiently: by controlling and influencing the customer's experience when they respond.

2. Service is a challenge.

You don't have to be a small-business owner to know that poor service is everywhere. As a customer, it's frustrating to have to deal with incompetence, laziness, lack of knowledge, aloofness, poor communication, or outright dishonesty when trying to give someone your money.

People are quick to blame the younger generation, but the problem is much larger than that. It includes individuals of every age group and background. Finding and keeping good employees who care about customers is the new holy grail of business, and every industry is in on the hunt.

What if the problem wasn't a generation, a group of parents, MTV, or the Internet, but a simple lack of applied focus on the part of the business owner to excite the employee about their responsibility to deliver value to each customer? How much does each individual employee know about how his or her contribution adds to the success of the organization? And more important, what's in it for them besides a paycheck?

Great service is remembered fondly by nearly every person who receives it. Growing businesses are obsessed with finding new ways of inspiring their people to deliver it.

3. Staff exposure to advertising is questionable.

How many of your employees have seen or heard your advertising?

---

* Information obtained at www.promomagazine.com/news/commercials_survey/index.html

Business owners make an enormous assumption that if they're running ads, their employees must surely see and hear them too. What business owners frequently forget is that the lives of many of their staff members are very different than that of their customers. Young people don't read newspapers often. Older people don't watch MTV. Commuters who ride the train rarely notice highway billboards. The people you hire to take care of your customers may not share the same interests, or media as the customers they serve.

If you've promised your customers something in your advertising, doesn't it seem logical that those who deliver the promise should know what it is? Ask yourself how closely your promise mirrors what actually happens when a customer experiences your company, either on the phone, online, or in person.

When your staff knows and understands the promise, there's a very real possibility they'll work to fulfill it for your customers, given the right set of incentives. If your people haven't been exposed to your advertising message, every single one of them is delivering *their* version of the promise instead of yours.

4. Customer expectations are high.

Today's customers—especially the Baby Boomers—are the fussiest, most demanding generation of consumers in American history. Whether it's in healthcare, fast food, lodging, or any other category, they have an overwhelming need to feel special and pampered, with little or no loyalty to any one particular vendor.

At the same time, every business category is fighting to be king of the hill in their standards of customer care, sometimes adding features and amenities costing many times what their return will be in order to keep up with the competition. When the innovation of the ATM became a competitive reality in banking, no bank wanted to buy these expensive machines because each one cost a fortune and literally contributed nothing to the bottom line. But when customers demanded this convenience, all it took was for one bank to take the plunge, and everyone else was forced to follow suit.

Every industry has its own version of the ATM, with thousands of changes in expectation and lifestyle that are challenging each of us to keep up. But since the conditions are not going away anytime soon, we must look hard to find the competitive business edges that aren't cost-prohibitive, yet can pay handsome dividends in customer satisfaction, repeat business, and positive word of mouth.

5. Employees don't like to be put in "unaware" situations.

How many of us like to feel stupid? Would you stay in a job that made you feel like you weren't very knowledgeable?

If you run ads promoting a certain product, and forget to tell your employees, that's just what they're going to feel like the moment a customer comes in and asks for the "advertised special."

"What offer?" asks the unsuspecting clerk. "I didn't hear about it."

Customers feel awkward. Employees feel out of touch. The trail of disappointed customers walking out of your business is a long, expensive one. And the line of staff members walking out in frustration is almost as long—and twice as expensive.

Worse, when the analysis of the offer is calculated, the only piece of data that exists is the number of units sold. If they didn't sell enough product during the campaign, the owner automatically assumes it must have been "something wrong with the advertising."

An informed staff is a happier, more stable, and more productive staff—especially when it comes to delivering on your promise.

6. Consumers are skeptical, and need confidence to buy.

Back in the early days of America, there were men in shiny suits selling bottles of snake-oil potion from the back of covered wagons. They stood on the back bumpers of their mobile platforms and guaranteed to the small crowd that their potions would "cure a host of illnesses, make an old woman young again, and grow hair on a bald man's head."

Too bad that group of people couldn't log on and Google snake-oil brands to compare their effectiveness.

But that's just what's happening today. Armed with a laptop, their neighbors' experiences, and a show-me attitude, today's consumers are the most skeptical group of buyers the world has ever known, relentlessly pursuing the truth in the products and services they buy through word of mouth, consumer reports, comparison Web sites, and any other means they can find. If there's a problem, they'll find it. If there's a better choice, they'll choose it.

If one of these "show-me" consumers finally makes it to your business through the multiple filters he's put up, his confidence level at the moment of purchase must still be high. There's still a chance that one of your employees could screw it up with a misplaced word or two, an indifferent attitude, or an uneducated answer to a question.

Customers are comparing everything—including your employees. How confident are your employees when dealing with customers? And how much confidence are they projecting to the customer that she made the right decision to buy from you?

7. A staff product endorsement is stronger than good advertising.

Go into any restaurant and ask the server, "What do you recommend on the menu?" The answer can be very telling. The server doesn't want to spoil her opportunity for a larger tip, so she had better tell the truth about the quality of a particular dish. Her answers are tacit endorsements, and they're usually taken very seriously.

Why is that? Because the restaurant guest knows that they can count on the server to be honest. The restaurant owner can brag about his all-you-can-eat fish fry in the newspaper all he wants, but the server has everything riding on the customer's meal experience.

What are your employees saying about your products or services when they're asked for *their* recommendations?

7a. A staff product endorsement is stronger than a manager's endorsement.

And while we're on the topic of perceived honesty, let's talk about the difference between an employee's response and the manager's response. Who does the customer believe will give the most honest answer to a question? That's right: the one who has less on the line. The manager is programmed by the owner, but the employee is the pipeline to "the real story."

What is "the real story" being told in your establishment today? And how are you maintaining it, polishing it, and making sure it's as good as it can be?

8. Repeat business is essential.

According to research from Jill Griffin and Michael Lowenstein in their book, *Customer Winback: How to Recapture Lost Customers – and Keep Them Loyal,* the average company can expect a sixty to seventy percent success rate selling more services to a current customer, compared to a twenty to forty percent chance of selling to a *former* customer, and a five-to-twenty-percent probability of making a sale to a *new* customer. Combine that with the fact that advertising is losing its effectiveness among these potential new customers, and you can see why it's becoming more important than ever to keep—and grow with—the customers you have.

Repeat business depends on many factors, including:

- Quality of the product or service
- Location
- Ease of purchase
- Price
- Continued need for the product or service
- Service received

If the competition claims superiority in one or more of these areas, repeat business is threatened. The good news is that you can control repeat business more effectively than you're controlling it today . . . by using your army of representatives—your staff—to their fullest potential.

9. Managers aren't always highly creative.

Every business needs good management, and each industry has its key indicators or qualities of their top managers. Unfortunately, creativity doesn't come in high on most of those lists. If you're a manager, who has time to be creative? You're putting out fires, hiring and disciplining, working on special projects (usually involving numbers), and doing a hundred other things, all with deadlines and urgencies.

One of the top qualities of effective *trainers*, however, is a good dose of creativity. To have the ability to reach someone through the right message delivered just the right way involves some creative-thinking power.

You've probably noticed that the best managers don't always make the best trainers. Give a manager a task, and she'll do it. Give a manager a complex problem like creating an effective, inspiring and engaging staff meeting, and you're likely to get one of those puzzled looks and a sideways tilt of the head.

If only the manager had a set of blueprints to work from, a guidebook that would lead the way in the form of exercises, ideas, and inspiration that were laid out exactly as needed for these cathartic staff meetings to happen. (Hey, we've got one of those for you! But we're getting ahead of ourselves.)

10. Time is NOT on the owner's side.

Have you noticed how quickly computers have been improving their speed and capacity? In the computer industry, Moore's Law states that at the current speed of advancing technology, the capacity of computer chips to store information will double every two years. So far, Mr. Moore's prediction has been right on. If you're in the computer-chip industry, time is NOT on your side.[§§§§]

And so it goes with the vast majority of other industries. Whatever business you're in, chances are you can't afford to wait until next year to improve. If you don't find ways to streamline, innovate, grow revenue, and cut expenses, someone else will . . . and there won't *be* a next year for you.

11. The fundamentals are important.

Every great sports team, every winning business plan, and every positive endeavor of any kind has at its core a group of simple tasks and skills that have been mastered. For those in a walk-in retail business, these fundamentals might include greeting customers, asking several core questions, finding and filling each customer's needs, and asking for his or her business again.

Just like ground balls and pop flies in baseball, these fundamentals must be repeated, drilled, and repeated again until they become so ingrained that they become part of each individual's personality. The fundamentals for each particular business must be salient (correct and prudent as it relates to the particular business), and repeated (to build familiarity beyond a shadow of a doubt).

Many employees think these things are boring, repetitive, and stupid. "No one really thinks we care, so why do we ask, 'How are you today?'" That's OK. These team members who think this way have a choice. They can jump aboard and prosper as a team, or they can take a walk across the street to their next job, where any old way of treating customers will do.

Salience and repetition. Salience and repetition. A fundamentally solid team is built by making sure the things that are done are the *right things*, and that they're done the *right way* each and every time.

Salience. And repetition.

[§§§§] Information obtained at *www.Intel.com/technology/mooreslaw/index.htm.*

12. Branding is the result.

The culmination of all we've talked about so far is that position in the mind and heart of the consumer that results in your name being first on the list when a need for your product or service pops up. Advertising is an important part of reaching people, but it's the experience that one has when the threshold of your business is crossed that will sear that brand indelibly in the minds of your customers.

Selling the Inside: How it Works

Selling the Inside involves training your staff on several elements of the business:

- *The Company's Advertising* — what's running now, where, and why

- *The Company's Sales Performance* — how we've done recently, whether or not we hit the goal we set, and what our goals are going forward

- *The Company's Service Performance* — a brief session on a single fundamental element of service at each staff meeting

Selling the Inside requires repetition, frequency, and consistency. Making time to communicate these things is also one of the most challenging aspects of business. You simply have to get ahead of the calendar and make training as routine as ordering product and paying bills.

Setting the schedule for training is the first step in getting everyone up to speed on your service plan. Whether you choose a weekly routine, a biweekly routine, or a monthly routine, it should be consistent. Nothing will backfire more than a program that is launched and not continued. If you start and don't follow through, your people will question your commitment. Much like your advertising, you have to set a plan and follow through.

These meetings will educate your team about your advertising message(s) and the team's goals, and will include a team exercise that will help them develop greater customer-care skills.

To maximize team meetings, we have created a sample outline. Here is how we suggest a typical meeting look:

I. SHOWCASE CURRENT ADVERTISING

A brief showcase of the advertising planned, including newspaper proof sheets, cable TV or radio ads to be played, photos of billboards, samples of direct mail, inserts, or any other marketing. This section should also include a short explanation about <u>why</u> this particular campaign was chosen.

II. DISCUSS THE FEATURES OF YOUR ADVERTISED PRODUCT OR SERVICE

In a team discussion, detail the features of your showcased product or service. Be sure to discuss the specifics on how the service or product is fulfilled and your promises, delivered. This step will require you to provide the passion, purpose, and pride behind what you are offering.

III. SCRIPT/TALKING POINTS

Create a few questions that will help you understand the needs of the customer. The goal is to give every member of the team the ability to respond intelligently to a customer who mentions the offer.

IV. REVIEW PAST PERFOMANCE

Incentives will help keep the team on track. Review last session's goals and discuss why the promotion was successful, or why it was *not*. Learn from past history.

V. REWARD PAST PERFORMANCE WHEN GOALS ARE MET

Reward met goals. Keep it simple, but make it genuine. Rewards don't have to be big to be perceived as having value.

VI. SET NEW GOALS

Set new goals to be measured by performance. For example, you don't want to make it a goal for everyone to try the new phone script. That is required, a goal is to sell x number of your featured program.

VII. SPECIFIC SKILLS TRAINING

This is the part where you bring your team further along in their ability to serve the customer. We believe that skill training is one of the most overlooked business growth opportunities. To get you started right away, we've included twelve excellent lessons for you to use in the Skill Module section in the back of the book.

Besides the obvious benefits of communicating your ad messages to the team, these meetings have several additional benefits, including:

- ◆ Understanding the importance of referrals to the overall health of the organization

- ◆ Reinforcing your commitment to the "Selling the Inside" Program to your team

- ◆ Allowing them to get to know each other better through the training sessions

- ◆ Providing a forum in which to learn from each other's insights and techniques

- ◆ Helping to identify future leaders in your organization

Your Staff and Your Advertising: Does One Know What the Other is Doing?

As you plan your meetings, it can be very helpful to understand how much your staff is aware of the messages you are sending.

If your people don't know <u>why</u> you're advertising, they won't feel as connected to the overall company mission, and may not have as much personal buy-in and passion for serving others.

If your people don't know <u>what</u> you're advertising, your team can't reasonably address any questions or problems that would arise regarding the ads, or talk as intelligently about the items that are featured.

If your people don't know <u>how</u> or <u>to whom</u> you're advertising, they won't be as prepared when the throngs of people come in or call.

The Advertising Awareness Audit is a tool to gauge just how much your team is aware of your current advertising, as well as an opportunity to learn their media habits. It's a simple questionnaire that you can use verbatim, change around, or use as a base upon which to build your own questionnaire. The results will allow you to gauge the amount of training needed given your particular staff and your particular market.

 **Free Goodie**

Want a printable PDF of the Advertising Awareness Audit? Go to the Goodie Box at *www.realitysells.com* and enter the word AAA in the box. Note: You will need to register if you are a first time user.

Reality Check:

Employee "Advertising Awareness Audit"

Employee: _____

Position/Job Title: _____ Today's Date: _____

Please answer each question completely and honestly. <u>There are no wrong answers</u>. The goal is to see where you stand today in your knowledge of your company's advertising, so that we know where to <u>expand</u> your knowledge to serve your clients in the best way possible.

CURRENT ADVERTISING PIECES:

(Please circle appropriate answer.)

I have seen AND READ a brochure from my company.   Yes/No

IF YES: Here's what I remember about what I read in the brochure about us:

_____

I have seen advertising for my company on TV.   Yes/No

IF YES: Here's what I remember about what I saw on TV about us:

_____

I have seen advertising for my company in the newspaper. Yes/No

IF YES: Here's what I remember about what I saw in the newspaper about us:

_____

I have seen advertising for my company on billboards.   Yes/No

IF YES: Here's what I remember seeing on billboards about us:

_____

I have heard advertising for my company on the radio.   Yes/No

IF YES: Here's what I remember hearing on the radio about us:

_____

I have seen or heard other advertising for my company. Yes/No

What kind(s) of other advertising have you seen
(or heard)? _____

Where did you see it (or hear it)? _____

What do you remember about it? _____

Do you know the advertising slogan or phrase that the company uses in its marketing?

_____

Think for a moment about the content of the advertising you've seen. In those ads, what did they say are the **main reasons why** someone should choose your company?

_____

_____

_____

What are the three main reasons that **you** think people should choose your company?

_____

_____

_____

How is your company <u>priced</u> compared to others in your community? (circle one)

On the higher-priced end/On the lower-priced end/In the middle/ Don't know

How does your company's <u>level of service</u> compare to others in your community? (circle one)

Better than average/A little lower than average/In the middle/ Don't know

ABOUT THE COMPETITION:

Who do you think is your company's biggest competitor in town?

_____

Why do you think they're your company's biggest competitor?

_____

_____

Have you seen or heard <u>their</u> ads?   Yes/No

IF YES: Where have you seen or heard them?

_____

_____

Would you be comfortable answering the question, "Why should I do business here versus your competition?"   Yes/No

How would you answer that question today if someone were comparing your company to your company's biggest competitor?

_____

_____

YOUR MEDIA CHOICES:

What newspaper(s) do you read?

_____

What radio station(s) do you listen to?

_____

What are your favorite TV shows?

_____

Do you have cable or satellite TV?

_____

Do you use IM (Instant Messaging) on your home computer?

_____

Do you use text messaging on your cell phone? Through which carrier? (Cingular, etc.)

_____

What did you think of this survey?

_____

Improving Sales Performance: Matchmaking

The one aspect of customer-service training that we continually hear from clients as the most difficult to overcome is salesmanship. They tell us their employees don't make the connection between customer service and sales. We believe that part of delivering excellent service is being able to suggest products and services to your customers that match their wants and needs.

Some people call this "sales."

Others would prefer to call it ANYTHING else.

A midsized regional bank needed to increase their deposits. Several senior managers had observed that their frontline tellers had developed excellent relationships with many of their banking customers, and suggested that the frontline tellers might be trained to sell new accounts, CDs, and other financial products. The rest of the team agreed, and decided to implement a frontline-sales program.

The team received extensive training on their products, and was given the words to use to begin "selling conversations" with their customers. An expensive sales-tracking software program was installed, and each team member was held responsible for asking a certain number of people to "buy" each week. To further encourage the best-possible outcome, each person was incentivized with a small commission for everything he or she sold.

It failed miserably.

Can you guess why?

There were several reasons:

1) The tellers didn't want to be salespeople.

2) They weren't instructed as to why it was important to the bank to make the change, so they felt out of the information loop.

3) The tellers didn't want to be salespeople.

Frontline staff members are typically employed in their position because it offers them a social environment, low risk, and a steady paycheck. If they wanted high risk and opportunity instead of security, they would have chosen mountain climbing or firefighting. Instead, they've chosen to do something comfortable instead of risky.

Sales scares them to death. Even if it may mean more money to them, they see negative value in becoming involved in something they despised as a consumer: being sold.

There's a fundamental rule at work here: People will do things when there's a benefit to themselves as well as the company. Certainly the company wins when the task is completed, but there must also be obvious value in it for the person who's doing the job. Possible benefits could be:

◆ Job security

◆ More money

◆ The ability to have more time off each week

◆ A better working environment (facility, coworkers, etc.)

◆ Something that's fun and exciting to them

Asking non-salespeople to sell assumes that the non-salespeople see value in it for themselves greater than the discomfort it may cause them. And that's where the bank got it wrong.

Non-Salespeople Will Sell . . .
if They Think They're Doing Something Else

Ask someone about their dog, their grandkids, or anything else that's dear to them, and they can ramble on lovingly for hours. Watch them pull the photos out of their wallet. Watch their eyes sparkle, their tone of voice elevate, and their enthusiasm rise to a higher level.

They think they're bragging about their loved ones. In reality, they're selling their grandkids to you.

They want you to feel the love and excitement that they feel. There's passion, sparkle, and sizzle in their delivery. They're thrilled to have the opportunity to share a part of who they are with you, because it makes them feel good and they believe it will make you feel good too.

How can you get your people to feel like that about selling your widgets?

There is a way. And it's much simpler than you think.

1. Remove the "S" Word.

To some people, calling someone a salesperson has one of the worst possible connotations in society. It's because nearly everyone has been ripped off at one time or another by someone with that title on their name tag. They trick people into doing things against their will. They are flim-flam artists—hucksters, and all they're after is your money.

There are many people in the workforce today who would become physically ill if their friends and family began to look at them as a "salesperson." It's the same to them as being labeled as someone without morals.

It's not true, of course. But that's the way many people feel.

Most entrepreneurs are natural salespeople, and so they have a hard time understanding why someone would feel this way. Even with monetary incentives that have the potential to change an employee's standard of living, the reality is that most people would rather run through the streets naked than have to sell something.

There's another reality that's equally fascinating: These same non-salespeople are the same people who help others to buy things all day long. They're selling every day. They just don't look upon it as "sales," and they may not be doing it as often as you'd like.

So in order to succeed at "Selling the Inside," we have to call this act of increasing the dollar volume and purchase frequency of the average customer something OTHER than "sales." Otherwise, it won't be a good mental fit with this sales-phobic group.

We suggest you call it something that most people can relate to: Matchmaking.

2. Introduce "Matchmaking."

All of us have met someone who's single and immediately thought of someone else of the opposite sex for whom this person would be PERFECT. This is matchmaking, and everyone can relate to "setting up" someone with someone else.

When a "match" is suggested, and a meeting takes place, how do they usually work out? It depends on a lot of things. If the stars are aligned just right, and if the matchmaker knows what he or she is doing in pairing people up, then the potential is good. If not, well, try, try again … perhaps with a match suggested by someone else.

It's the same thing in sales.

When we're a prospect looking for a product or service to buy, we're a lot like a single person. We have a want or a need, and we're looking for a "match." If a company employee recognizes that need, can ask the right questions, and can suggest the right "match" for the particular situation, that's matchmaking.

Except that most managers just call it by its recognized name: selling. Your stuff, their need.

This kind of matchmaking doesn't always turn out favorable, but the process is still very important in determining the right "match."

Here's a real-world example: A young lady is looking for a new car. She has a certain set of criteria, and she goes to the dealership looking for a particular model. The salesperson spies her in the showroom, engages her in conversation, and begins the dance:

"Is this the only color you have?"	"What color are you interested in?"
"Does it come with a sunroof?"	"Yes, it does. Is that important to you?"
"What's the resale value?"	"I have information here. Would you like to see it?"
"Does it corner well?"	"Would you like to take it for a test-drive?"

The young lady is a little scared of making a wrong decision, paying too much, not seeing enough of the other models available, etc. The salesperson knows which questions to ask that will help her decide whether or not the car is the right one for her. Sometimes there's a match, and sometimes not.

Sound familiar?

If you can succeed in getting your staff to think about sales as matchmaking, you will help to eliminate the single biggest roadblock to their success: shedding the mentally unacceptable social label of being a salesperson.

3. Educate on the available "matches" in your product lines.

So how does a matchmaker go about making a match?

Let's imagine that Andy and Bill are going to open up a matchmaking service. Our first objective would be to compile a database of our "inventory"—the single men and women who have contacted our service—and learn as much about them as we can:

- Their physical description
- Their likes and dislikes
- Their goals in finding a match

After we get know our "products," it's time to go out and identify those other single men and women who would be a good "match" for the others in our inventory. We would need to ask them a series of similar questions regarding:

- Their physical description
- Their likes and dislikes
- Their goals in finding a match

We would have to get to know them a bit better so we could assess their compatibility with the dozens of people who are available in our database. We might think we see a match right away, but we would need to ask a few more questions before we suggest anyone from our inventory, because we want to make as few matchmaking mistakes as possible.

We would then put the information into the computer, and show them a few of the matches that came up. Then we would ask them if they would like to become happily involved in our dating service.

If they say yes, the deal is done. The service will benefit both parties; it's a win-win situation.

Should we be angry, upset, or disappointed if someone says no? Not at all. If it's not right for them for whatever reason, we don't want them to make a wrong decision. If he or she is interested, they'll come back at a later time when it feels right. It probably wasn't something personal, but we may never know for sure.

This is sales!

You learn your products.

You learn what kinds of people can use the products you have.

You then look for "matches"—people who fit the description of those who can use the products.

You ask them if they'd like to see if there's a match between their needs and what your products can do for them.

If they like it, and it fits, everybody's happy.

If they don't, it's no big deal. You don't take it personally. Maybe the next situation will be a match.

You dust yourself off, and look for the next opportunity.

4. Keep looking for matches.

Getting to know your products is the only true way to excel at matchmaking within your company. You must know the details of what you offer inside and out, so that you can answer each question intelligently and lead your "potential match" toward the answer you're looking for.

The most difficult part of this kind of work for most people is the constant rejection that happens. Hearing the word "no" multiple times a day isn't the most pleasant part of someone's work life. However, if you look at it as matchmaking, one man may find Girl A very attractive, and Girl B rather plain Jane to him. Does it mean that Girl B is never going to find happiness in her life? Of course not. Just because he didn't like Girl B doesn't mean that there's not another attractive young man out there who's going to fall head over heels for her.

It's up to the customer to make the decision. You're giving all the information needed to say yes or no based on your knowledge of the products and the customer's personal situation. If the answer is no, it could be for a hundred different reasons. You've done the best you could in matching them up. And that's what you do. If they say no, it isn't because you didn't hold up your end of the bargain.

Let's say you find a perfect match, but the relationship takes an ugly turn and blows up. Does that mean you should give up matchmaking? No! This sort of thing happens every day, with businesses large and small in every corner of the globe. Just because one relationship didn't work out doesn't mean you have to become something else. In fact, some of the lessons learned from mistakes along the way can be some of the best education you can receive.

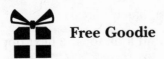 **Free Goodie**

Want more tools on how to turn your front line staff into happy, productive matchmakers? Go to the Goodie Box at *www.realitysells.com* and enter the word MATCHMAKING in the box. Note: You will need to register if you are a first time user.

CHAPTER 7
The Center of the Compass:
Acting Deliberately

The center of the compass is the base of each direction. On our compass, the center holds the Law of Acting Deliberately.

The way in which you approach Freedom, Originality, Repeatability, and Transparency is just as important as the Laws themselves. If any of these Laws are approached in a way that appears contrived, insincere, or with an ulterior motive, they will come across as such, and with the opposite effect than what you had planned.

In order to act deliberately, everyone must know and believe in your overarching purpose for being in business, and that message must be communicated consistently to all the stakeholders. A one-time shot of information in a meeting is not enough. It is not effective in creating long-term knowledge, branding, and buy-in of the purpose. Habits are formed through consistent, deliberate training and repetition of the desired message or activity over time.

Being deliberate encourages a sense of purpose, enhances productivity, and supports decision making. Lack of deliberateness creates indifferent companies.

Acting Deliberately means that all actions and words must be entered into with a specific goal and purpose in mind.

The four Laws are only effective when approached in earnest. Go out in public, and it is easy to find countless examples of half-committed people. That's why is so delightful to see examples like the Cathy Family of Chick-Fil-A, Jimmy Liautaud of Jimmy John's, Roy H. Williams of Wizard Academy, and Mark Cuban of the Dallas Mavericks. These people are passionate and take the time to get the little things right.

People are afraid that creating a culture where systems are rigorous will lead to boredom and squash the creativity out of the organization. But it doesn't have to be this way. You can create rewards for performance that encourage people to go above and beyond, and have a good time along the way. Chick-Fil-A is known to supply cars to people who meet lofty goals. Jimmy John's doles out watches and motorcycles. Telling people why things are done *the way they are* also helps keep people engaged, when they understand why, they will start coming to you with ideas and suggestions on how to be better.

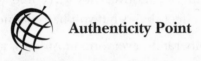 **Authenticity Point**

If you are trying to change the culture of an organization, then everything you do, including the smallest detail, needs to be done with a strong dose of deliberateness. New ideas that are half implemented will cause people to revert to the old way of doing things, or worse, create their own way.

The Leader's Role in Authenticity

As a leader, there are three key concepts that bring substance to your leadership. They are:

Passion — The life the business or organization is built upon. It's what's in the veins.

Purpose — The role the business is filling in the life of the customer.

Pride — The quality standard at which the business operates.

A structure with three points of support is very strong and stable; if you master them, these three will be reflected throughout your business.

Passion

Passion is an addictive quality that pours energy into the business. It's like the bass line of your favorite song: driving and pulsing, it brings you along. People find passion attractive, and it's like love; the more you give away, the more that comes back. Passionate people often have followers, and passionate businesses usually have raving fans.

Are you and your staff excited about what you do?

Purpose

Why are you in business? The reason you get up and go to work is to make money, but in the long run, you must have a keen understanding of the role you are playing in the life of the customer. Does your work have meaning to the customer?

What purpose does your business fulfill in the lives of those you serve?

Pride

Are you confident in what you do? Do you set standards that show you care about the business? From having a store that is clean and well stocked, to having well-trained staff, you have to show that you believe in your business. Taking time to train your people on the rudiments of customer service embodies the principles of pride. Without passion or purpose, pride is a more difficult mountain to climb.

Does your staff exude the pride you feel for your business?

When all three are working together, there is incredible energy and synergy everyone can feel. Leaders make this kind of synergy happen.

 **Authenticity Point**

All the great leaders I know have been able to contagiously live with passion, speak with purpose, and serve with pride. Would you want to follow the opposite?

CHAPTER 8
Reality is a Journey that Leads to Authenticity

Our study of authenticity has led us to meet many people, learn from some amazing companies, and most importantly realize that the process of continual improvement is ongoing. If we could summarize our findings to date, they would be:

♦ To achieve the greatest degree of long-term success, a company's advertising must be Authentic, with a clear consumer advantage, a message that connects the advantage to the business, and enough frequency to generate activity on the part of the consumer.

♦ The advertising has to be clearly understood by both customers and staff in order to gain the maximum degree of return on investment.

♦ For maximum ROI, the staff must also have knowledge of what is being advertised and how (TV, newspaper, direct mail, radio, etc.). The customer experience must match or exceed the expectations laid out to the customer in the advertising, and the surest way to make this happen is to make sure the staff knows what's being advertised and how.

♦ Ongoing training in basic customer service, sales, and operational skills must be conducted continuously to assure that frontline staff and line-level managers are equipped to fulfill the promises made in the company's advertising.

- ◆ A staff's lack of knowledge of service basics, sales basics, operational basics, or the current ad campaign can lead to damaged reputation, negative word of mouth, lost sales, and negative cash flow.

- ◆ The best strategy a business owner can employ is to communicate frequently with his/her staff on the current advertising plan, share the objectives of the campaign with them, and make them active participants in its success.

- ◆ Since the campaign's success is ultimately tied to delivery of the promises made, the business owner should frequently train the staff on the basics of good customer care.

- ◆ Leadership that has integrity, lives with passion, speaks with purpose, and serves with pride can make an enormous difference when it comes to being real.

The future of this project has already begun. We would like to invite you to join us. For more information, visit *www.realitysells.com.*

CHAPTER 9
Bonus Materials:
Skill Modules

Selling the Inside doesn't happen by accident; it takes a pre-planned effort on your part, and a willingness to improve on the part of your team. But we also recognize that planning takes precious time – something you may not have in abundant supply,

We've created these Skill Modules for you to help save some time in creating effective and productive team meetings. Use these Modules as part of the Specific Skills Training that we suggested in the Selling the Inside Team Meeting outline on Page ___. Feel free to modify, enhance, or improve any and all of them. They are creative exercises to get your team to begin thinking about the essentials of good, fundamental customer care.

Skill Module #1:
Creating "Wow, You Noticed!" Moments

To each customer, the most important person in the world is THEM. This exercise will help your staff to recognize the importance of noticing—and commenting positively on—a unique detail of a customer. Any transaction can be routine; a "Wow, You Noticed!" Moment can actually lift someone's spirits for the entire day!

TIME NEEDED: 8–12 minutes

YOU WILL NEED: No supplies needed

THE EXERCISE:

LEADER: Tell the group to quickly pick a partner for this exercise. (If there is an odd number of people, choose the "odd man out" to be *your* partner.)

Turn and face your partner, and tell the group that your assignment is to look at your partner for eight seconds, and find something about him or her that you admire and you know they're proud of. It could be something they're wearing, their hair, their purse, whatever. Immediately give the signal, "Go!" Count off eight seconds silently, then say, "Time's up!" Have each person turn from their partner and face you.

Go around the room and quickly find out from several participants what they "found."

LEADER: Ask the group:

◆ How do you feel when someone gives you a genuine compliment about something?

◆ Do you know when someone is "faking it"? Do you know when someone is complimenting you in a forced or insincere way?

◆ When we're sincere about our customers, it shows. Sometimes we become so busy each day, we fail to notice the "little things" about our customers of which they're very proud. Their tie, their hair, their car, their ring, their coat, their pets—each of these things is very personal, and can be the source of great pride if someone takes the time to notice it.

◆ It's also good for *us* to try to notice those things. Why do you think it's good for us to do that? (Good answers: "It keeps us alert and watchful," "It keeps us focused on the customers instead of other distractions around us.")

◆ What is it about your next customer that noticing it would make her smile and think to herself, "Wow, you noticed!"? (Go around the room and ask people to list things that they've noticed about other customers.)

◆ How do you think this simple change would affect the opinions of some of our customers about us as a place to do business?

◆ Let's go and make someone's day today, by noticing the little things about others!

LEADERS—SOME HELPFUL HINTS FOR THIS EXERCISE:

Let your people know that not every customer has something to compliment. Don't force it. If you don't find something particularly appealing about a customer, then just go about serving them. If your comment is not genuine (authentic), don't say it!

Acceptable compliments might include:

"Your coat looks nice and warm."

"That's a gorgeous ring! I love the color."

"I love your purse! Do you like it?"

"Is that a new cell phone? I've never seen one like that!"

Compliments to avoid (you can use these examples for a little bit of humor):

"That's a really nice toupee."

"I haven't seen a car like this since my mom drove one!"

For the eight-second exercise, you may wish to prompt your group about what kinds of things you would like noticed, to avoid any embarrassing situations. Before starting the exercise, you might create a short list of four to five things, and read it out loud prior to starting the "eight-second timer."

There will be some people who do not talk at all. That's OK. For some people in the room, this will be their first experience with this kind of dialogue. Allow them to absorb the information at their pace. Even though they may not be talking, there's still learning going on.

Skill Module #2:
Answering Customer Questions

Every business is bombarded with questions from customers every day. In this exercise, you'll be discussing the most frequently-asked questions, and how those questions should be answered by everyone on the team.

TIME NEEDED: 15–20 minutes

YOU WILL NEED: Paper and pencil for each employee White board or large easel

THE EXERCISE:

LEADER: Ask each team member to choose a partner for the exercise, then tell this story:

- The cast members at Walt Disney World in Florida are asked thousands of questions each day. "Which rides have longer wait times in the afternoons?" "When does the park open tomorrow?" "Where's the bathroom?" and others.

- Some of them are a little bit strange. One of the most frequently-asked questions at Disney is, "What time is the 3:00 parade?" Now, if you were a Disney employee, how would you be tempted to answer that? (Take answers from the group; silly answers are OK.)

- Here's how Disney trains their people to answer: "Well, the parade usually starts on time, but it's best to get a seat about twenty minutes early. Would you like to know where some of the best spots are to watch the parade?"

◆ The Disney cast member added value to their answer for the guest. He or she made them feel like their question was a VERY intelligent thing to ask! In fact, not only do they know what time the parade begins, they know how they can make the most of their parade experience.

◆ What would happen at OUR place if someone were to ask a question like that?

(Take brief answers from the group for a few moments, then move right into the next paragraph:)

◆ Anytime someone asks you a question, it's because they honestly need the information. It's important not to make them feel stupid, no matter how odd their question is.

◆ What questions are *we* asked most frequently at *our* company?

(Motion to pencil and paper, and demonstrate to the group.)

◆ Get with your partner right now. I'd like each of you to draw a line dividing the page into two halves, left and right. For the next three minutes, I'd like you and your partner to write down some of the common questions we get here at work, whether it's on the frontlines, on the phone, or anywhere. Discuss those questions, and write them down on the LEFT-hand side of the paper.

(Allow three minutes or more for team members to write down their answers.)

◆ OK, what are some of the questions you've written down?

(Go through several of the questions one by one; write each of them on the easel just as it's read to you. Address <u>why</u> someone might have that question, and <u>how</u> you <u>could be</u> answering that question positively.)

LEADERS—SOME HELPFUL HINTS FOR THIS EXERCISE:

Some groups will be prone to make up stupid questions that would NEVER come up in a real customer situation. Keep the questions "real," and make sure that the person who states the questions writes down the best answer he or she heard from the group.

Have everyone turn in their papers at the end of the exercise, and have someone type up all the responses. Save in a file for future reference, and/or tack onto the back wall for the week.

Whether or not everyone participates, everyone will have learned something in this exercise.

Skill Module #3:
The Top-11 Reasons List

In this exercise, you'll be asking your employees their opinions about why customers ought to choose you. You'll learn about their current pool of knowledge of your company, if their perceptions are right or not. Allow them to correct each other about the benefits of doing business with you.

TIME NEEDED: 20–25 minutes

YOU WILL NEED: Paper and pencil for each employee White board or large easel

THE EXERCISE:

LEADER: Have everyone number a piece of paper from one to eleven, then ask each to write across the top: THE TOP-11 REASONS TO CHOOSE (your company name).

- ◆ I'd like you to take five minutes to write down what you believe are the Top-11 Reasons to choose our company as someone to do business with.

- ◆ They can be reasons that people choose it today based on feedback they've heard, or reasons that people don't know about that are perhaps under-advertised.

◆ Work independently, and we'll talk about your answers once they're done.

After the five minutes are up, ask a team member to come up and be the scribe. Go around the room in any order you like and ask each employee to read their list one by one. Have the scribe write down each unique answer, avoiding duplicates, until each team member has had a chance to contribute. **Don't comment on the answers**; just write them down.

Next, divide the group into two to four teams, and direct them in this way:

◆ For the next five minutes, this half of the group (either one or two teams) is to look at the list, and decide among the group which of the items are the five <u>most important</u> things that we should be telling people in our advertising.

◆ The other half of the group's assignment is look at the same list, and decide as a group which of the items are the five <u>least-known</u> reasons why people <u>should</u> be doing business with us.

After five minutes are up, choose a spokesperson from each team to read their list aloud and defend their choices. Allow positive discussion back and forth, if it should break out.

Questions to ask the team:

◆ What did you learn?

◆ Is it a good idea to know why someone does business with you? Why?

◆ What can we do as a team to make sure we communicate these things to our current customers?

◆ Is our advertising saying the right things to people who aren't our customers yet? If not, what directions should we consider?

Thank them for helping to educate each other on the major benefits of choosing your company. Let them know that it's the sharing of knowledge like this that will allow all of us to serve our customers better and help each of us to grow.

LEADERS—SOME HELPFUL HINTS FOR THIS EXERCISE:

Keep the discussion positive at all times. This is not a session designed to criticize your current marketing campaign or your weaknesses as a company.

Keep the master list of reasons that you generate, and consider typing it up for everyone to have, including the two top-five lists. If there's a place to post things, consider posting that list for a short time as a reminder to the team of what was discussed.

Skill Module #4:
Do Others Think You're Honest?

In this exercise, each team member will be awakened to the impact they make on each other with the first impression they give, especially with their eye contact. It's easy to forget that the impact we make on each other isn't just with customers; it's with those we work with as well.

TIME NEEDED: 15–20 minutes

YOU WILL NEED: Paper and pencil for each employee White board or large easel

THE EXERCISE:

LEADER: Ask each team member to choose a partner for the exercise. Ask them to introduce themselves if they don't know their partner well, and choose who will be Partner A and who will be Partner B. Start this discussion:

♦ Talk this question over with your partner: <u>What do you notice about people who are not being honest or</u>

---

straightforward with you? A's go first; then each partner alternates giving an answer. Write down all your answers on your sheet of paper.

Allow 2–3 minutes for the partners to discuss the question and write down their answers. *Potential answers: No eye contact, fidgety, shifting their weight from one side to the other often, looking around nervously, uninterested, talking fast, distracted, overly angry, fake laughter or talk.*

Once the two minutes are up, ask everyone:

◆ What was your number-one answer?

Most will say, "Can't look you in the eye" as the number-one response. Write it on your big easel or whiteboard, and ask the group:

◆ Why did you put eye contact as number one? (Get answers from the group.)

◆ What other answers did you come up with?

Write down their other answers underneath "eye contact" on the left side of your large white board.

Next, ask the group to get together with their partners again and answer this question:

◆ What do you notice about people who ARE being honest with you? B's go first this time, and alternate with their answers, writing them down once again.

Give them two minutes to finish this exercise. Then ask for responses and write them on your white board on the right side.

Look over the two lists side by side, and then ask the group this series of questions, encouraging their response and participation:

◆ How is the second list different from the first list?

◆ How important is it that our customers perceive us as being the most HONEST place with which to do business?

◆ What might happen if the customers somehow thought we were being dishonest with them?

◆ What can we do as a team to make sure that EVERY customer feels comfortable in doing business with us?

Thank them for their responses, and encourage them to remember that others are judging us every day for our honesty.

LEADERS—SOME HELPFUL HINTS FOR THIS EXERCISE:

Be careful not to make this appear as a "witch hunt" for dishonest employees! This is NOT the reason for the exercise. It is to recognize what actions or gestures that OTHERS (customers and coworkers) may recognize as potentially dishonest, and to consciously remove those activities that might lead to distrust.

If groups have difficulty coming up with a good list, help them with one or two examples from the list above to get them started in the right direction.

Skill Module #5:
Owning a Piece of the Business (In Your Mind)

In this exercise, your team members will all become qualified to become "owners" of the company, and be encouraged to think differently about the work they do.

TIME NEEDED:	10–15 minutes
YOU WILL NEED:	A number of chocolate or bubble-gum cigars (enough for at least one per team member)
	An "Official Certificate" (created on your own or copied from the Certificate/Worksheet on the following page)

THE EXERCISE:

LEADER: Ask each team member to pick a partner for this exercise. When partnering is completed, pass out copies of the "Official Certificate," tell each team member to print their name on the first line, and sign it at the bottom.

Address the team in this way:

◆ You've all just become qualified "owners" of the company, and that you've got cigars for everyone to celebrate your new "ownership." (Pass the boxes or jars around, and let each team member pick one cigar on their own.)

◆ Congratulations! What's the first thing you're going to do as an owner? (Typical answers: "Eat this cigar," "Give myself a day off," or "Give myself a raise.")

◆ You might say, 'GIVE MYSELF A RAISE' . . . OK. Only now, you're going to have to figure out how you're going to pay for yourself.

◆ Instead of giving yourself a raise, what if you received five dollars for every one hundred dollars in business we did tomorrow? Would it suddenly become more important to you that every customer was treated well?

◆ If you got a piece of every transaction that was done, would it mean more to you that the place was clean and neat? That each phone call was answered with courtesy and respect? That everyone looked his or her best on the job?

◆ What do you notice about people who work as if they owned the place? What characteristics do they have? (Move on to the next bullet before anyone can answer)

◆ You've probably seen someone moving around quickly and skillfully in a restaurant or somewhere else, doing several things at once, and said to yourself, "Wow! That person works like they **own** the place!" It's the ultimate compliment you can give someone else.

◆ People like Oprah Winfrey, Martha Stewart, and Donald Trump are famous "owners." What do they do differently than others? What characteristics do they possess that others can see?

Ask the group to then answer that question with their partner for three minutes or so, using the bottom part of their Certificate/ Worksheet or a blank sheet of paper.

Possible answers: *Owners are self-confident, risk-takers, hard-working, take action, quick to give out praise to their team, accept personal responsibility, resourceful, come up with solutions to problems.*

After a few minutes of work, ask the group to share some of their responses out loud. Tell the group that if they hear something that they like that they didn't think of, that they should write it down and add it to their list. Give public praise to those who come up with good answers.

Then address the group in this way:

◆ Take another look at the list you have, and think about this for a moment. **Could all those words on your list be descriptions of YOU?** (Pause a few seconds to let everyone reflect on their answers.)

◆ In order for us to continue to grow and thrive as a company, we all need to take OWNERSHIP of what we say and do each day. If we all were to do all these things that owners do, we would improve greatly as a team and as a company that serves others greatly.

◆ Will you all think more like an OWNER today . . . and every day? (Get an OK from the group.) Thank you!

LEADERS—SOME HELPFUL HINTS FOR THIS EXERCISE:

This can be an excellent exercise, but it can easily get off track! Make sure you have a good command of the group, and that they are not locked into a current battle with you about wages, hours, etc. The "ownership" analogy can backfire with the wrong attitudes in the room!

Skill Module #6:
Frequently Asked Questions . . . and How to Answer Them

Every business receives a number of the SAME questions each day. How we respond to them is critical in building a positive rapport with customers. In this exercise, your team members will better understand that customer questions are important, and should be treated that way, even if it's the 25th time they've been asked the same thing.

TIME NEEDED: 10–15 minutes

YOU WILL NEED: Paper and pencil for each employee White board or large easel

THE EXERCISE:

LEADER: Ask the group to choose a partner, and determine who will be Partner A and who will be Partner B.

Then lead the discussion this way:

◆ The cast members (the word they use for "employees") at Walt Disney World in Florida are asked thousands of questions each day. "Which rides have longer wait times in the afternoons?" "When does the park open tomorrow?" "Where's the bathroom?" and others.

◆ Some of them are a little bit strange. One of the most frequently asked questions at Disney is, "What time is the 3:00 parade?"

◆ Now, if you were a Disney employee, how would you be tempted to answer that? (Take answers from the group; silly answers are OK.)

◆ Here's how Disney trains their people to answer: *"Well, the parade usually starts on time, but it's best to get a seat about twenty minutes early. Would you like to know where some of the best spots are to watch the parade?"*

♦ Instead of rolling their eyes and saying "Oh brother, another stupid-guest question," the Disney cast member answered it politely and actually added value to their answer for the guest. He or she made them feel like their question was a VERY intelligent thing to ask! In fact, not only do they know what time the parade begins, they know how they can make the most of their parade experience.

♦ What would happen at OUR place if someone were to ask a question like that? (Take brief answers from the group for a few moments, then move right into the next paragraph.)

♦ Anytime someone asks you a question, it's because they honestly need the information. It's important not to make them feel stupid, no matter how odd their question is.

♦ What questions are <u>we</u> asked most frequently here at our company?

Motion to pencil and paper, and demonstrate to the group:

♦ Get with your partner right now. I'd like each of you to draw a line dividing the page into two halves: left and right. For the next three minutes, I'd like you and your partner to write down some of the common questions we get here at work, whether it's at the front counter, on the phone, or anywhere. Discuss those questions, and write them down on the left side of the paper.

Allow two to three minutes for team members to write down their answers. Then ask:

♦ OK, what are some of the questions you've written down?

Go through several of the questions one by one; write each of them on the easel just as it's read to you. For each answer, respond in this way:

- Why would someone have that question?

- How could we answer that today? Could we be more positive in our answer?

- What ADDITIONAL value could WE add to the answer WE give in the same way that Disney gives the parade answer?

Discuss the meaning of body language, and even though the team may be using the right words, their silent message could be sending the wrong signals. For example, rolling the eyes, huffing and puffing, crossing the arms, tilting the head back, and other physical things can lead someone to believe that their question is bothersome to you, even though you're saying all the right things.

- One other thing to remember: This goes not only for your customers, but ALSO for your coworkers. There are no stupid questions, and we cannot treat each other any differently than we would our best customers. We're a TEAM.

- Thanks for participating; our customers will come back more often if we can answer each of their questions like this!

LEADERS—SOME HELPFUL HINTS FOR THIS EXERCISE:

Some groups will be prone to make up stupid questions that would NEVER come up in a real customer situation. Keep the questions "real," and make sure that the person who states the questions writes down the best answer he or she heard from the group.

Have everyone turn in their papers at the end of the exercise, and have someone type up all the responses. Save in a file for future reference, and/or tack onto the back wall for the week. Use the sheet at a future weekly meeting, and see if the questions have changed since you conducted the meeting the last time.

Whether or not everyone participates, everyone will have learned something in this exercise!

Skill Module #7:
Creating New Habits

When training people on a new system, method, or procedure, old habits are difficult to break. In this fun exercise, your team members will learn that change is difficult because of the "ruts" in our brains created from doing the same things over and over again in the same way. These "ruts" need to be retrenched, and that takes effort from everyone.

TIME NEEDED: 8–10 minutes

YOU WILL NEED: A bath-sized towel

Additional materials to illustrate a change you've recently made that you want everyone to adopt. (See notes at end of exercise.)

THE EXERCISE:

LEADER: Ask the team to partner up in groups of two. Begin the session by saying this:

◆ Today we're going to start off with a demonstration.

Choose someone from the team to volunteer to stand in front of the group for the demonstration.

◆ We're going to talk today about things we do every day that we don't even think about.

Get the bath towel, hold it by one corner so that it falls open to its full length, and present it to the volunteer.

◆ (Volunteer name), would you please show us how you dry yourself off when you get out of the shower or bath at your home?

They will look shocked at first, but encourage them in a good-natured way.

◆ Where do you start? What part of your body gets dried off first? (Encourage them to pretend that they just stepped out of the shower, and to use the towel to dry off that part of their body that they would begin to dry off first.)

◆ Do you always start there? (Wait for answer.) OK . . . where do you go to next? (Wait for answer.) Then what?

When the exercise is through, thank the volunteer and ask the group to give him or her a round of applause. Then begin by asking the group:

◆ Do you do the same thing every time you get out of the shower? Do you start with the same area each time? Would it be weird for you to start somewhere else, like your feet first?

◆ You've been doing it for so long, you don't even THINK about it now. It just happens.

◆ What scientists know now is that we actually create RUTS in our brains from doing the same things over and over again. There are physical ruts, like tiny trenches, that we've burned into our brains that automatically do some of the things that we've repeatedly done.

◆ Here's another demonstration that will help you understand the concept: Clasp your hands in front of you so that your fingers are interlaced and one thumb is on top of the other.

◆ Now, unclasp and re-clasp your hands so that the OTHER thumb is on top.

The group will say that the new grip feels "weird," "unnatural," and "funny."

◆ That's what starting a new habit is like. You have to understand that your human nature is going to say, "This isn't natural." You have to overcome your natural tendency to remain comfortable, and that's why doing new things is so difficult.

HERE IS WHERE YOU INTRODUCE THE NEW PROCEDURE, POLICY, OR ACTIVITY YOU'VE INTRODUCED. EXPLAIN WHY THE CHANGE WAS MADE, THE ACTIVITY YOU WANT, AND THE ACTIVITY YOU WANT TO ELIMINATE.

Then say:

♦ Just like the shower and when folding your hands, I recognize that change is difficult. But you'll need to feel uncomfortable at first, so that NEW "ruts" in your brain can be burned, and this new system is as automatic as the old system was.

LEADERS—SOME HELPFUL HINTS FOR THIS EXERCISE:

The towel portion of the exercise can be embarrassing for some of your team members. Choose a volunteer that you know can mentally accept a little self-deprecation.

Decide which new activity you want to talk about prior to the session, and be prepared with any materials you need to pass out to further illustrate your demonstration of the "new" way to do the activity.

Skill Module #8:
Questions to Ask While You're Answering
Their FIRST Question

Successful companies understand that what people ask for may not be exactly what they need. In this exercise, your team members will learn that part of their role as customer-service providers is to save the customer the hassle and embarrassment of making a wrong purchase decision.

TIME NEEDED: 10–15 minutes

YOU WILL NEED: Paper and pencil for each employee
White board or large easel

THE EXERCISE:

LEADER: Ask your team to pair up in teams of two, then tell this story:

A young manager of a small home-electronics retail store noticed a customer coming into the store late in the evening, about ten minutes before closing time. She asked the customer if she could help him find something. "Yes, I need a clock radio, please," he said.

"Right this way," she said. On the way to her store's display of clock radios, she asked him politely, "What will you be using it for?"

He explained that he was new in town, and that his first day of his new job was tomorrow morning. He needed a clock radio to be sure that he woke up on time.

"Well, if you're new in town, and don't have a clock radio, you might be in need of a few other things," she suggested. "Do you have a TV yet?" He said he did not. She asked about several other things her store carried, many of which the man needed.

Thirty minutes later, the man walked out with over $2,000 in purchases . . . just because an enterprising young manager had the foresight to ask a simple question: "What will you be using it for?"

Ask the group these questions:

- Was it wrong of her to ask that kind of question?

- Would the man have made those purchases at some point in the future?

- Is there a chance that he would have bought them somewhere else?

- What benefits did the man receive by buying them from her that he may not have received somewhere else?

- How many items would the man likely have purchased if the manager had NOT asked him the question?

- How can WE go about doing the very same thing here?

Ask your team to divide into groups of two, and answer this question on a piece of scratch paper: **Why is it a good idea for us to ASK customers about their reasons for buying a particular product?** Give them two to three minutes to come up with answers.

Possible answers might include: Reduces the chance of the customer buying the wrong item, and wasting time having to return to the store; increases the chance of upselling; engages the customer in positive conversation; moves us closer to the perception of being helpful experts in what we do.

When two to three minutes have expired, ask several teams to share their best answers with the group.

Then ask each team to discuss this follow-up question: **What words can WE use to ask customers about their purchase requests?** Give them an additional two to three minutes to consider and write down their answers as a two-person team.

Write down the best answers on a large easel or whiteboard, and say to your group:

- I'd like each of you to memorize these words. These are excellent conversation-starters that lead to BETTER purchases, FEWER returns, and HAPPIER customers.

- Thanks for participating, and let's hear more conversations with our customers!

LEADERS—SOME HELPFUL HINTS FOR THIS EXERCISE:

Some groups may not be able to come up with acceptable answers. That's OK; use the suggestions from some of the stronger groups, and the weaker groups will learn from their suggestions.

If the group is not moving in the direction you'd like, use one or two examples as thought-starters for them.

Skill Module #9:
Waiting – and What it Does to Customers

Our perception of time is different when we're doing something we enjoy versus when we're waiting for something. In today's society, our patience is thinner than ever, and most people grow angry quickly when forced to wait for anything. In this exercise, the concept of waiting is discussed, and the team will learn that everyone needs to be mindful of any length of time that customers are waiting, and make their wait as enjoyable as possible.

TIME NEEDED: Approx. 15–20 minutes

YOU WILL NEED: A clock or watch with a mechanism for telling the seconds

A whiteboard or easel

THE EXERCISE:

LEADER: Begin by telling the group that you will be watching the clock or your watch, and that you want the entire group to be completely silent. When you give the word, each individual will sit silently and wait for what they believe is sixty seconds. When each person believes that sixty seconds has passed, they are to say the word "Time!" out loud. (Have them close their eyes if there is a clock on the wall, or have people cover their watches or cell phones with their hands.) AS THE LEADER, DO NOT CALL OUT WHEN SIXTY SECONDS HAVE PASSED.

After about ninety seconds, say:

◆ Why didn't everyone say "Time!" all at once?

◆ It's because everyone's perception of time is different . . . especially if we're waiting for something.

◆ How many of you felt like that exercise went on forever?

♦ Wherever people are today—on the phone, in their cars, or waiting in line—people are much more annoyed about waiting than ever before. Why do you suppose that's happening?

Possible answers may include:

♦ Because of high-speed Internet, e-mail, faxes, instant messaging and FedEx, people are used to things happening instantly.

♦ People are busy and don't have time.

♦ People have higher anxiety levels today, and waiting adds to stress.

♦ They're overbooked and can't afford to waste a minute.

♦ Everything else is instant, so waiting seems old-fashioned.

♦ There's always someone else who can serve them more quickly at another place.

♦ Do you think it's harder to please customers today because of this expectation of instant service?

♦ What's the longest you've ever waited on hold on the phone? Who did you call? (Get responses, have them tell one to two stories.) How did you feel while you were on hold?

Now, begin to move the discussion from other places to YOUR place:

♦ Why do people have to wait at our place?

♦ Can we reduce the number of times that people have to wait to be served? How?

♦ What could WE do with our customers to make their waiting experience more enjoyable, less stressful, or even more fun?

Write down the first seven to eight suggestions, no matter how ridiculous. Then look at the list and ask the group:

♦ How many of these things could we do TODAY, without a major remodeling or needing to buy anything extra?

Circle those things. Then ask the group:

♦ Can we make ONE of these happen today?

Put a star next to that item, and get agreement from the team that the action can indeed happen today.

Then ask:

♦ Since everyone hates to wait, and we all agree that whatever we can do to cut down the amount of waiting time would benefit our customers, can we all do our very best today and all this week to see if this ONE action will cut down on our customers' waiting time?

Get agreement from the group, reinforce the group's decision, and thank them for moving the idea forward. Adjourn the group.

LEADERS—SOME HELPFUL HINTS FOR THIS EXERCISE:

Some suggestions for reducing or eliminating the stress of waiting might be:

♦ Serve a beverage, snack, or warm cookies to people who are waiting.

♦ Have a TV or other diversion in the waiting area, e.g., video games, etc.

♦ Offer to allow people to use the restroom without losing their place in line (perhaps by using a number system).

♦ Make a telephone or computer available.

♦ Have current reading materials available, or offer the latest newspaper or magazine.

♦ Offer mini-massages, shoe polishing, or other perceived luxury amenity.

♦ Have a kids' play area where waiting takes place, so parents aren't stressed with having to entertain their children for long periods of time.

◆ Offer certificates for nearby restaurants or coffee shops for customers to be used while they wait. (You might be able to do a trade with someone.)

Skill Module #10:
The Power of First Impressions

TIME NEEDED: Approx. 15–20 minutes

YOU WILL NEED: An easel or whiteboard

THE EXERCISE:

LEADER: Begin by asking this question, and write their answers on the left side of your easel:

◆ You're going on a blind date with someone. What would be something about your blind date that would make a BAD first impression on you?

The list your group comes up with might include:

- ◆ Physical appearance
- ◆ Clothing
- ◆ Posture
- ◆ Facial expression
- ◆ Personal hygiene
- ◆ Cologne/Perfume
- ◆ Bad listener
- ◆ Bad attitude
- ◆ No eye contact
- ◆ Handshake ("limp fish")

- No smile

- Nonstop talker

- Now take a look at this list. Aren't these the same kinds of judgments we make about those we do business with too?

- Great first impressions aren't just for attracting the opposite sex. They're also good business techniques.

- Have you ever decided NOT to go to a restaurant because of the way it looked on the outside? How about the inside? The servers? The smell?

- How about a first impression that you get over the PHONE?

- It's estimated that sixty-eight percent of customers have their first contact with a company over the phone. How many of you have made a decision NOT to buy from a particular store after your FIRST phone conversation with them?

- What are some of the things you notice about companies that have GREAT people answering the phone? (Make another list on the easel)

The list should include things like:

- A smile in her voice

- Helpful and not rude

- Knowledgeable

- Easy to understand

- Good attitude

- Not distracted by others while talking to you

- Makes you feel like your call wasn't a bother to her

Reinforce the "blind date" concept by asking this:

- Aren't our customers calling us for a "blind date" over the phone?

◆ Many people who call are shopping for a place where they feel comfortable . . . and the phone is the first place they're likely to go.

◆ Whether it's on the phone or in person, we want to make a positive first impression EVERY TIME!

Ask your team to consider every encounter with a customer as though it were a potential "blind date" . . . to smile genuinely, make eye contact, engage them in good conversation, and win that customer over.

LEADERS—SOME HELPFUL HINTS FOR THIS EXERCISE:

Some of the younger groups may make this line of conversation a sexual-innuendo fest. As the leader, you must keep the group on track, and continue to use the metaphor of "wooing" a potential customer in a non-raunchy way.

You may wish to focus on first phone impressions OR first in-person impressions separately, so that the group can think about improving one of them at a time.

Skill Module #11:
"On-Stage" vs. "Off-Stage"

This Disney-inspired concept is critical to those who work on the floor with customers. Occasionally, employees find themselves talking to each other or to other customers in ways that are too personal for others to be comfortable around. After this session, your team should be able to instantly recognize what areas of the operation are appropriate for personal conversations to take place.

TIME NEEDED: Approx. 15–20 minutes

YOU WILL NEED: A drawn map of the retail or service area of your business on an easel or whiteboard that's easy for everyone in the room to see (It doesn't have to be fancy, but should be fairly accurate.)

THE EXERCISE:

LEADER: Begin by talking about the underground system of tunnels at Disney:

◆ About fifty years ago, Walt Disney had a problem

◆ One day, while walking around and observing things at his Disneyland theme park in California, Walt noticed a cowboy character walking to work in his cowboy outfit through Tomorrowland. The space theme and the cowboy outfit clashed, and Walt didn't want his guests to see that . . . so he fixed the problem when he built his park in Florida.

◆ At Walt Disney World in Florida, there is a system of underground tunnels and rooms that the guests never see. It's an underground city, complete with parking garages, cafeterias, and everything you'd expect to support the cast members— the employees—who work there.

◆ There are a series of hidden entrances throughout the park that people go in and out of from this underground area, so you'll never see a Disney employee in an area that isn't exactly where they should be.

◆ All of the costume changes, all of the prep work, all of the personal conversation that goes on between cast members takes place underground or in designated areas called "Off Stage." When each cast member goes "On Stage," everything is about serving the guests. No costume adjustments, eating, talking to one another, or other similar activity is to happen in an "On Stage" area.

◆ You'll NEVER hear a personal conversation between two cast members at the top of Space Mountain! That's an "Off Stage" conversation, and is only held in designated areas.

Gesture to the map of your store or business, and ask a volunteer to come up to the easel. Give them a pointer, or something similar, and say:

◆ Here's a map of our "Stage." Let's look at this for a moment. Where would you say would be OUR "Off Stage" areas—those places that it would be OK to eat or change, or to hold a personal conversation? Point to those areas. (Allow the volunteer to point to the areas; if they need help from their teammates, that's OK.)

◆ OK. Take a look at that map again. Are there places that personal conversations are taking place today that are within the range of customers' ears? Where are those areas? Point them out to me. (Allow the volunteer to point out those areas once again. Others will want to chime in and help.)

◆ Are there some things being said or talked about in our "On Stage" areas that should NEVER be taking place in front of customers?

Answers should be along these lines:

◆ Talking about the last customer who left (their odor, clothing, etc.)

◆ Being judgmental or gossiping about anything

◆ Talking about other employees in front of customers

◆ Talking about their love lives

◆ Their family situations

◆ Their "lousy job"

◆ Anything else OTHER THAN their job at hand, which is to serve the customer!

◆ What could be the result of someone overhearing one of those conversations?

Possible answers:

- ◆ Negative word of mouth about the company to others

- ◆ Customer won't return, because she doesn't want to be the subject of your NEXT conversation after she leaves!

- ◆ Lost future business

- ◆ Loss of job as a result

- ◆ Potential Lawsuits (libel, slander)

Designate the volunteer as the official "Sign Post-er," and give them two signs that say "Off-Stage Area" and "Entering On-Stage Area." Say this:

- ◆ If I were to ask you where should these signs go, where would you put them? (Allow them to point to the places on the store map where they should go.)

- ◆ I'd like to ask you to put them there right after we're done today. Does everyone understand this, and understand why it's important?

- ◆ Let's truly work on making sure that everyone sticks to this concept. We don't want customers to feel badly about us, and we want to concentrate on them . . . so please put those signs up, and let's make sure that conversations that belong "Off Stage" stay there.

LEADERS—SOME HELPFUL HINTS FOR THIS EXERCISE:

Not everyone will get it, and the old habits of many of your people will slip back immediately after this session. It may be helpful to assign key people to monitor and point out to others when a conversation or other activity is an "Off Stage" action versus an "On Stage" action.

Skill Module #12:
The Importance of Name Tags

Many resort destinations have discovered that a nametag creates a sense of comfort with customers that few things can match. In this exercise, your team will see what kind of power a name tag can wield, and how their name tag actually helps them to do their job with a higher degree of confidence.

TIME NEEDED: Approx. 10–15 minutes

YOU WILL NEED: "Hello, My Name is . . ."–style stick-on name tags (enough for one for everyone in the group)

THE EXERCISE:

LEADER: Begin by asking people to pair off into groups of two. Once they've each found a partner, ask this question:

- Has anyone been to Las Vegas lately? (Get responses.)

- For those of you who have, most every name tag in Las Vegas has two things on it. Do you remember what those two things are?

Their first name and their hometown.

- Why do you suppose they have those two things on them?

It initiates conversation about where they're from.

- Do you suppose that a New Yorker coming up to the blackjack table might take a look at a name tag that says, "Phil— Brooklyn, NY" and decide to sit down because there was a kindred spirit dealing the cards? Is there a good chance that he'll start a conversation with Phil about his hometown?

- Name tags break down conversation barriers between two people. With name tags, people begin to enter into fearless, meaningful dialogue.

Ask the group if they've ever had trouble remembering someone's name. Immediately ask them if a name tag could have relieved the stress of that moment.

♦ Name tags allow people to talk to one another without fear of forgetting who it is they're talking to.

Hospital employees wear name tags for several reasons, but one of the primary reasons is because they want patients and families to feel comfortable about addressing them by name. A hospital can be a stressful place, and remembering your nurse's name is just one less thing to worry about.

Pass out the blank name tags, and ask each person to do this exercise:

♦ I'd like for you to write down something OTHER than your given name. Just like in Vegas, we want people to feel good about coming in and being with us. So right now, I'd like for you to create a DIFFERENT name tag for yourself. Perhaps it's the name your grandkids call you . . . like Nana or Mammaw. Maybe it's a nickname you had in college . . . like Mongo or Crazy Legs. Maybe it's something you're very proud of . . . like Master Gardener or Easy Rider.

Take a few moments now and come up with your own name tag for yourself, then put it on and share with your partner why you chose that name. (ALLOW CONVERSATION BETWEEN PARTNERS.)

After about one minute or so, ask for a few volunteers to tell the group what their PARTNER'S name tag says. Enjoy a few good moments of discovery among the group, then ask this question:

♦ What would be the harm in wearing that exact name tag at work today?

♦ What might happen if you were to wear it? Would it cause people to immediately smile and feel better?

◆ Would people ask about your name tag? Would it start an interesting conversation?

School food-service workers have used these name tags, and have called themselves such things as "Jessica, the Vegetable Queen," "Frieda, Master Gardener," and "Mrs. Breese, Super Scooper." You may wish to try that and see how it works with your team.

Ask your group to wear the name tag they've created on their next shift. Begin to use them more often, and they'll be surprised at the conversations they begin.

LEADERS—SOME HELPFUL HINTS FOR THIS EXERCISE:

Guide your team toward name tags that will help others to smile. A little self-deprecation is OK, but keep the name tags on the upbeat side. "Bill the Loser" is probably not a name tag you'll want to encourage; however, "Bill—Piano Man" says something about Bill that might not have been known by anyone else.

For more helpful information on name tags and their power, go to Scott Ginsberg's site, *www.HelloMyNameIsScott.com.* Scott is the king of the name tag, having worn a "Hello My Name is"-style name tag for several hundred days in a row and cataloguing all that has happened to him as a result.

Index

WIN WEALTH WORTH WITH WBUSINESS BOOKS

Sales

First 100 Days of Selling: A Practical Day-by-Day Guide to Excel in the Sales Profession
By Jim Ryerson
ISBN 13: 978-0-8329-5004-9
Price: $22.95 USD

Soar Despite Your Dodo Sales Manager
By Lee B. Salz
ISBN 13: 978-0-8329-5009-4
Price: $19.95 USD

Great Salespeople Aren't Born, They're Hired: The Secrets to Hiring Top Sales Professionals
By Joe Miller
ISBN 13: 978-0-8329-5000-1
Price: $19.95 USD

Hire, Fire, & the Walking Dead: A Leaders Guide to Recruiting the Best
By Greg Moran with Patrick Longo
ISBN 13: 978-0-8329-5001-8
Price: $19.95 USD

Marketing

What's Your BQ? Learn How 35 Companies Add Customers, Subtract Competitors, and Multiply Profits with Brand Quotient
By Sandra Sellani
ISBN 13: 978-0-8329-5002-5
Price: $24.95 USD

Entrepreneurship

The N Factor: How Efficient Networking Can Change the Dynamics of Your Business
By Adrie Reinders and Marion Freijsen
ISBN 13: 978-0-8329-5006-3
Price: $19.95 USD

Thriving Latina Entrepreneurs in America
By Maria de Lourdes Sobrino
ISBN 13: 978-0-8329-5007-0
Price: $24.95 USD

Millionaire by 28
By Todd Babbitt
ISBN 13: 978-0-8329-5010-0
Price: $19.95 USD

Check out these books at your local bookstore or at
www.Wbusinessbooks.com

THIS BOOK DOESN'T END
AT THE LAST PAGE

Log on to **www.WBusiness.biz** and join the WBusiness community.

Share your thoughts, talk to the authors, and learn from other community members in the forums. **www.WBusiness.biz** is a place you can sharpen your skills, learn the new trends and network with other sales professionals.

DATE DUE

OCT 1 1 2007

GAYLORD   PRINTED IN U.S.A.